Operation Cobra 1944

Breakout from Normandy

Operation Cobra 1944

Breakout from Normandy

Steven J Zaloga · Illustrated by Tony Bryan

Series editor Lee Johnson · *Consultant editor* David G Chandler

First published in Great Britain in 2001 by Osprey Publishing,
Midland House, West Way, Botley, Oxford OX2 0PH, UK
443 Park Avenue South, New York, NY 10016, USA
Email: info@ospreypublishing.com

ISBN-10: 1-84176-296-2
ISBN-13: 978-1-84176-296-8

CIP Data for this publication is available from the British Library
Editor: Lee Johnson
Design: The Black Spot
Index by Alan Rutter
Maps by The Map Studio
3D bird's-eye views by Encompass Graphics Ltd.
Battlescene artwork by Tony Bryan
Originated by PPS Grasmere Ltd., Leeds, UK
Printed in China through World Print Ltd.

Typeset in Helvetica Neue and ITC New Baskerville

06 07 08 09 10 13 12 11 10 9 8 7 6 5 4

FOR A CATALOGUE OF ALL BOOKS PUBLISHED BY
OSPREY MILITARY AND AVIATION PLEASE CONTACT:

NORTH AMERICA
Osprey Direct, C/o Random House Distribution Center,
400 Hahn Road, Westminster, MD 21157, USA
E-mail: info@ospreydirect.com

ALL OTHER REGIONS
Osprey Direct UK, P.O. Box 140,
Wellingborough, Northants, NN8 2FA, UK
E-mail: info@ospreydirect.co.uk

www.ospreypublishing.com

Author's Note

The photographs in this book, unless otherwise noted, are
official US Army Signal Corps photos. They were found at
several archives including the US National Archives in
College Park, Maryland, the Special Collections at the
US Military Archives at West Point, New York, the Military
History Institute at the US Army War College at Carlisle
Barracks, Pennsylvania, and the Patton Museum at
Ft. Knox, Kentucky. The author would especially like to
acknowledge the kind help of Alan Aimone, Special
Collections, US Military Academy; Randy Hackenburg of
the Military History Institute; and Charles Lemons and
Candace Fuller of the Patton Museum in locating material
used in this book.

Artist's note

Readers may care to note that the original paintings from
which the colour plates in this book were prepared are
available for private sale. All reproduction copyright
whatsoever is retained by the Publishers. All enquiries
should be addressed to:

Tony Bryan
4a Forest View Drive,
Wimborne,
Dorset
BH21 7NZ
United Kingdom

The Publishers regret that they can enter into no
correspondence upon this matter.

KEY TO MILITARY SYMBOLS

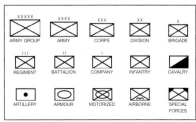

CONTENTS

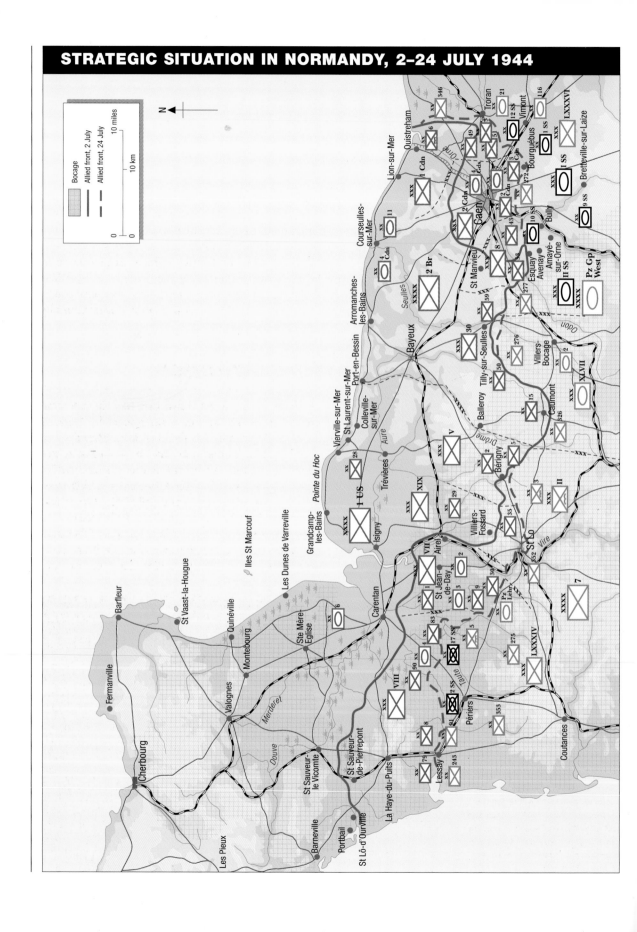

STRATEGIC SITUATION IN NORMANDY, 2–24 JULY 1944

Bocage
Allied front, 2 July
Allied front, 24 July

0   10 miles
0   10 km

N

INTRODUCTION

One of the most decisive months of World War II was the thirty days between 25 July 1944 and 25 August 1944, starting with Operation Cobra, and ending with the liberation of Paris. By the end of August, German forces in Normandy were utterly destroyed, and the remaining German forces in central and southern France were in headlong retreat to the German frontier. The following month, Allied forces liberated much of Belgium and the Netherlands, and penetrated the Siegfried line into Germany. Operation Cobra fundamentally improved the prospects for Allied victory.

THE STRATEGIC SITUATION

In mid-July 1944 Allied forces were bogged down in a bloody stalemate in Normandy. The British 21st Army Group, commanded by General Bernard Law Montgomery, had attempted a series of tank offensives to break out of the salient near Caen. Montgomery had hoped to seize the city shortly after the June invasion, but had been frustrated by the skillful German defense. Caen finally fell on 10 July 1944, but the next effort to break through the tenacious German defenses on 18 July 1944, Operation Goodwood, was a costly failure. The difficulties in the British sector were all the more worrying as the original Allied plans of May 1944 had assumed that Montgomery's forces would take the lead out of Normandy due to their closer proximity to the German frontier. The area around

Operation Cobra was conducted in the bocage, a type of dense coastal hedgerow. The hedges were so thick that they created a natural fortification line for the defender. Here, a rifleman of the US 29th Division has cut a firing hole through a hedge during the fighting along the Vire river on 7 August 1944.

LEFT **Nowhere was the bocage more claustrophobic than along the boundaries of two properties. These were often separated by two hedgerows, creating a trench between them. They made ideal defensive positions like this one near Carillon.**

BELOW **The capture of the key road junction at St. Lô was vital to the American plans for Operation Cobra. The city finally fell on 18–19 July, setting the stage for the offensive. In the ruins of the city is a German SdKfz 231 armored car. This was a relatively old type of reconnaissance vehicle that had been largely replaced with the more modern SdKfz 234 series by the time of the Normandy campaign.**

Caen opened onto rolling countryside, suitable for mechanized operations, while the American sector to the west was less suitable.

The First US Army, commanded by General Omar Bradley, had its share of frustrations as well. Allied planners had seriously miscalculated the tactical implications of the terrain in the American sector. The area near the coast was boggy, exacerbated by the summer rains in July. Further inland the terrain quickly turned into *bocage*, the French term for coastal farmlands bordered by hedgerows. The hedgerows had grown dense over the centuries, the local farmers clipping off branches for firewood, and leaving a thick bank of roots and earth, three or four feet high. The bocage was ideal for defense, forming a band of natural fortification unsuitable for maneuver. It undermined the US Army's firepower advantages since the hedgerows provided natural protection against artillery and air attack. The Germans skillfully exploited the bocage, defending the sector field by field.

9

Nevertheless progress had been made, notably the capture of the port of Cherbourg at the end of June. An assault towards Coutances had been halted, but the First US Army reached the outskirts of St. Lô by mid-July. Frustrated at the failures in the British sector, Bradley began to consider the possibilities of a breakthrough in the American sector. The outline of what would become Operation Cobra began to take shape in early July 1944. Bradley recognized that for a mechanized advance to succeed, it would be necessary to advance beyond the bocage into the more open country south of St. Lô. Instead of the broad advance that had been characteristic of the American operations in June and early July, Bradley decided to stage the breakthrough on a narrow front by a single corps, with the corps on either flank keeping the German forces tied down. The original Overlord plan for the Normandy invasion assigned Bradley's forces the task of seizing the ports in Brittany. The key objective of the Cobra breakthrough was the city of Avranches, the gateway to Brittany. By initiating Cobra near St. Lô and swinging west towards Avranches, the offensive could also trap a large portion of the German Seventh Army. Bradley's plans were supported by intelligence reports that suggested that the German army in Normandy was near breaking point.

For the Germans the strategic situation was grim. The summer of 1944 had seen the entire Eastern Front collapse in a series of catastrophic Red Army offensives. The Soviet forces had struck in three successive phases. The first offensive crushed German defenses around Leningrad and in Finland and the Red Army surged forward along the Baltic. The most destructive was the June offensive in Byelorussia, codenamed Operation Bagration [see Campaign Series 42], which destroyed Army Group Center. The success of Bagration pushed the Red Army into central Poland and allowed the launching of another offensive towards Lvov and Sandomierz in July that unhinged the southern wing of German defenses in the east. The Red Army poured into the Balkans, and Germany's main source of oil was soon threatened. The situation in the Mediterranean theater was bleak, with Rome falling in June 1944. The successful defense of the Normandy bridgehead through the middle of July was one of the few bright spots in the strategic picture.

CHRONOLOGY

6 June: D-Day Landings. Allied forces land on the northern coast of Normandy.

22–27 June: Battle for Cherbourg. The port is eventually captured but is so badly damaged as to be useless for some considerable time.

3 July: US First Army begins to attack southwards towards St. Lô. The dense nature of the bocage country results in very slow progress and heavy casualties.

8–11 July: British and Canadians launch Operation Charnwood. They break into Caen but fail to clear the entire city.

17 July: Field Marshal Erwin Rommel, commander of Army Group B, is severely wounded when his car is attacked by RAF ground-attack aircraft. Von Kluge takes over direct command of Army Group B.

18 July: Operation Goodwood begins. Caen is cleared but gains are limited. Goodwood does succeed in concentrating German attention on the British sector however.

18 July: St Lô is finally taken by the Americans.

20 July: Hitler survives an attempted assassination at the "Wolf's Lair", his forward command post in East Prussia. This intensifies Hitler's suspicion of the German officer corps.

24 July: Carpet-bombing attack scheduled to begin at 13.00hrs is cancelled. Some of the aircraft do not get the message and carry out the attack. US 30th Division suffers more than 150 casualties from bombs that drop short.

25 July

09.36hrs: P-47 fighter-bombers begin strafing runs and ground-attack missions along the northern edge of the bomb zone. They are followed by more than 1,800 heavy bombers which carpet bomb an area 7,000 yards long by 2,500 yards deep. The effect on Panzer Lehr Division is devastating. US troops suffer approximately 600 casualties from bombs dropping short, including LtGen Lesley McNair, head of US Army Ground Forces.

11.00hrs: VII Corps begins ground assault but advance is held up by areas of continued resistance. US forces only penetrate about a mile.

24.00hrs: Town of Hébécrevon is finally taken.

26 July: MajGen Collins of VII Corps orders his armored units to spearhead his advance. German defenses begin to collapse as CCB/3rd Armored Division and 1st Infantry Division capture Marigny and 2nd Armored Division advances seven miles.

28/29 July: German forces in the Roncey pocket are largely destroyed while trying to break out.

30 July: MajGen John Wood's 4th Armored Division seizes Avranches.

31 July: Key bridge at Pontaubault captured without resistance by task force from 4th Armored Division.

1 August: First US army becomes 12th Army Group and Gen George Patton's Third Army is activated. 4th Armored Division halted by determined resistance at Rennes airport.

2 August: Luftwaffe attempts to destroy bridge at Pontaubault in night attacks using guided missiles. The attacks fail.

3 August: During the night the garrison of Rennes abandons the city.

5 August: CCA/4th Armored Division reaches Vannes on Quiberon Bay.

7 August: CCB/4th Armored Division reaches outskirts of Lorient.

5 August: Initial attack by 83rd Division on St Malo.

Night of 6/7 August: Operation Lüttich, the German counterattack at Mortain, begins. 2nd Bn., 120th US Infantry, surrounded on Hill 317, continue to call in artillery on the German forces.

7 August: Attacks begin in earnest on St Malo. Task Force A joins with 6th Armored Division on the outskirts of Brest. Garrison of Brest does not surrender until 19 September.

8 August: Patton's troops liberate Le Mans. First Canadian Army launches Operation Totalize aimed at Falaise.

12 August: In a daring night attack Leclerc's French 2nd Armored Division seize the bridges over the River Sarthe.

13 August: Bradley orders Patton to direct his corps east rather than north into the Argentan-Falaise gap.

14 August: St Malo is finally taken after intense house-to-house fighting.

15 August: US Seventh Army lands on the southern coast of France near Marseilles.

16 August: The Canadians finally take Falaise, leaving a gap of only 15 miles between the Allied spearheads. Hitler finally agrees to the withdrawal of German units in the Falaise pocket. Patton's Third Army is on the outskirts of Chartres and Orléans.

17 August: Von Kluge is replaced by Generallfeldmarschall Walter Model. Von Kluge commits suicide the next day. Citadel of St. Malo finally surrenders after direct fire from 8-in. guns from a range of only 1,500 yards.

21 August: Falaise pocket is finally sealed. 10,000 German troops have been killed and 50,000 captured in the pocket, whilst 313 tanks have also been lost.

23 August: Hitler informs the commander of the Paris garrison, Dietrich von Cholchitz, that the city "must not fall into the hands of the enemy except as a field of ruins."

25 August: French and US troops including Leclerc's 2nd Armored Division liberate Paris.

THE OPPOSING COMMANDERS

Generalfeldmarschall Guenther Hans von Kluge commanded both the OB West and Army Group B during the Cobra operation, posts that had previously been held by Rundstedt and Rommel. (MHI)

On 20 July 1944, days before Operation Cobra, a group of German army officers attempted a coup against Hitler in his forward command post in East Prussia, the "Wolf's Lair". Hitler survived the bomb blast, and the coup attempt quickly collapsed. The plot had a corrosive effect on the subsequent German operations. As the deputy chief of operations, Walter Warlimont, later recalled "[Hitler's] actual injuries on 20 July had been minor but it seemed as if the shock had brought into the open all the evil of his nature, both physical and psychological." Already distrustful of the German officer corps, the coup only intensified this anger and made Hitler suspicious of all but the most obsequious commanders. Any officer who dared to question his genius in the art of war was suspected of treason. Not only did Hitler insist that German positions be held no matter the cost, but he demanded the German army launch counteroffensives under the most inauspicious circumstances. Hitler's worsening mental imbalance deprived German field commanders of vital tactical flexibility.

Hitler's appreciation of the strategic picture in the west was poor. Into late July he still believed that Normandy was a secondary operation and that the Allies planned their main amphibious landing in the Pas de Calais. This mistaken assessment was widely shared by senior Wehrmacht commanders, and stemmed from the natural advantages that the Pas de Calais offered as well as Allied deception operations. Although Hitler grudgingly allowed the transfer of panzer divisions from the Pas de Calais to Normandy, badly needed infantry divisions were hoarded until too late. German intelligence during the summer of 1944 was poor, and in July the Foreign Armies West section concluded that the Allies would not launch an amphibious assault into southern France. In spite of this assessment, Hitler refused to move many of the fresh divisions in the Bay of Biscay and Mediterranean areas to Normandy. The same "hold-fast" mentality limited the transfer of divisions out of peripheral areas such as Norway.

Prior to Cobra Erwin Rommel was injured during an air attack and was in the hospital. Sitting next to him is Paul Hausser, who commanded the Seventh Army during Operation Cobra. (MHI)

The key Allied commanders in Normandy were Dwight Eisenhower, head of Supreme Headquarters Allied Expeditionary Force, and Bernard Montgomery, commander of Allied ground forces and of the 21st Army Group. Here they are seen in a relaxed mood after a meeting on 26 July, a day after the start of Operation Cobra.

The major American commanders during Operation Cobra were present for this group portrait. In the first row (left to right), George S. Patton, Omar Bradley, Dwight Eisenhower, and Courtney Hodges. In the second row, William Kean, Charles Corlett, J. Lawton Collins, Leonard Gerow, and Elwood Quesada.

The German position in Normandy in July 1944 was further undermined by Hitler's frequent dismissals of senior commanders. The German armed forces in the west were under the direction of the OB West (*Oberbefehlshaber West*). Generalfeldmarshall Gerd von Rundstedt had commanded this higher headquarters until 2 July 1944 when he was relieved by Hitler for proposing to withdraw German forces to more defensible positions in Normandy out of the range of naval gunfire. **Guenther Hans von Kluge** replaced Rundstedt. Kluge was one of Hitler's favorites, having commanded the Fourth Army during one of Germany's greatest feats of arms during the war, the envelopment of the French forces through the Ardennes in 1940. Kluge had a distinguished record on the eastern front, but was seriously injured in an automobile accident in October 1943. In contrast to the aloof and aristocratic Rundstedt, the younger Kluge was a far more dynamic leader, frequently visiting the front line units. Kluge was a traditional Prussian officer who was nicknamed "Clever Hans" for his political opportunism and tendency to vacillate. He was aware of earlier plots against Hitler and was privy to the 20 July plot. Suspicions about his loyalty were raised when the Gestapo interrogated one of his former aides. Shortly after receiving news that the coup had failed Kluge had sent an obsequious telegram to Hitler pledging his loyalty. During the Normandy fighting in late July 1944 Kluge worried that his marginal role in the plot would result in his arrest.

There were two army groups in France in July 1944, Army Group B under Field Marshal Erwin Rommel and Army Group G under Colonel General Johannes Blaskowitz. Rommel's Army Group B included the Seventh Army opposite the Normandy beachhead, the Fifteenth Army holding the Pas de Calais, and the First Parachute Army occupying central France and Paris. The much weaker Army Group G consisted of the First Army on the Bay of Biscay and Nineteenth Army on the Mediterranean coast. Rommel was seriously wounded on 17 July 1944 when a Spitfire strafed his staff car. He was implicated in the 20 July plot, but was offered the chance to commit suicide, which he did in October to save his family. After a difficult time with Rommel, Kluge took over direct command of Army Group B in late July 1944.

Seventh Army was split in two to allow better direction of the Normandy campaign. The reconstituted Seventh Army was opposite the American sector of the front, and the new Panzer Group West was responsible for the British and Canadian sector. The Seventh Army had been commanded by Colonel General Friedrich Dollmann, who died of a heart attack on 29 June 1944. He was replaced by a veteran panzer commander, **SS Colonel General Paul Hausser**, who had led II SS Panzer Corps. Both Rommel and Rundstedt had opposed his appointment preferring a more experienced Wehrmacht officer. Hausser was a professional soldier who had earned the Iron Cross in World War I and retired from the Reichswehr in 1932 as a lieutenant general. He became involved in Nazi party politics, and because of his past military background, he was involved in the formation and training of the early Waffen SS formations. So he was sometimes called "the father of the Waffen-SS". By 1944 he was 64, 13 years older than his American counterpart, Omar Bradley.

Corps command in Normandy had remained more stable. Hausser's Seventh Army consisted of two corps, the 84th Corps under **General**

The key American tactical commander during Operation Cobra was J. Lawton "Lightning Joe" Collins, who led VII Corps. His decision to promptly commit his armored exploitation force was critical to throwing the German defenses off balance. (USMA)

George S. Patton and Omar Bradley relax in August following the successful execution of Operation Cobra. Patton proved the ideal commander for the exploitation operations that followed Cobra, and his dynamic leadership was instrumental in the race to the Seine in mid-August.

Dietrich von Choltitz, and the 2nd Parachute Corps under Luftwaffe **General Eugen Meindl**. Choltitz had begun the war in the Polish campaign as an infantry battalion commander, rising to divisional commander in August 1942 and to corps command in December 1942. He had won the Knight's Cross for his battalion's performance in France in 1940. Although a Luftwaffe general, Eugen Meindl was a paratroop officer and took command of the other corps of Seventh Army due to the significant proportion of paratroop divisions in this sector. Meindl had been an artillery officer in World War I, serving in mountain artillery at the outbreak of World War II. He switched to the Luftwaffe paratroop force in 1940 and had his first combat jump in the 1940 landing at Narvik. His unit took part in the costly landings at Crete in 1942. He was decorated with the Knight's Cross and his skilled leadership led to his appointment as a Luftwaffe corps commander in November 1943.

The Allied counterpart of the German OB West was SHAEF (Supreme Headquarters, Allied Expeditionary Force), headed by **General Dwight Eisenhower**. Eisenhower's tutelage under the flamboyant head of the interwar army, Douglas Macarthur, helped prepare him for a role that demanded diplomatic skills as much as military experience. Eisenhower had caught the eye of the US chief of staff, General George C. Marshall, while a young colonel on the war plans staff at the beginning of the war. Compared to his German counterparts, Eisenhower encountered significantly less political interference from higher authorities. Eisenhower's main challenge stemmed from the difficult nature of coalition warfare, especially in balancing American and British interests.

The senior ground commander in Normandy was **General Bernard L. Montgomery**, who served as commander of the 21st Army Group. Eisenhower's problems with Montgomery had less to do with his abilities than his personality. His briefings to Eisenhower prior to the British offensives in June and July were full of grand expectations, but when the plans went awry he redefined the goals to try to redeem the failures. He later asserted that the primary role of the offensives was to tie down German panzer forces to permit an American breakout, when in fact the Allied plans had expected the breakout from the British sector. Not only

Allied airpower provided a crucial ingredient in the success of Operation Cobra due in no small measure to the tactical innovations of the commander of the 9th Tactical Air Command, MajGen Elwood "Pete" Quesada, seen here with Omar Bradley.

did the failures around Caen undermine his reputation among American commanders, but his tactless remarks about the inexperience of the US Army and its leaders laid the seed for later controversy.

General Omar Bradley commanded the First US Army in Normandy, and was subordinate to Montgomery until the creation of the US 12th Army Group on 1 August 1944. Bradley had been a classmate of Eisenhower's at the US Military Academy at West Point in the class of 1915. Like Eisenhower he had not served in combat during World War I, though he had served in the Mexican border war in 1916–17. He had distinguished himself as an infantry officer in the interwar army, and attracted the attention of George C. Marshall while an instructor at the infantry school in the early 1930s, and again while working on the General Staff in 1938. After raising the 82nd Division, he served as deputy commander of II Corps under General George S. Patton in North Africa in 1943. In Sicily Bradley served as a corps commander, again under Patton's command. Bradley and Patton had known each other from the 1920s when they had both served in Hawaii. They were a complete contrast in style and temperament – Bradley the son of a poor Missouri sodbuster, and Patton from a wealthy family with a long military tradition. While Patton's star waned after Sicily, Bradley's rose. Patton's decline began with an incident on Sicily where he slapped some shell-shocked soldiers for cowardice. Eisenhower had found Patton to be impetuous and difficult to control during his command of Seventh Army on Sicily. Bradley, in contrast, had proven himself to be an able and competent corps commander, if not so bold as Patton. Patton was unable to keep his foot out of his mouth, and after further impolitic outbursts to the press in England his career went into hibernation, making Bradley the choice to lead in France.

In July 1944 the First Army in Normandy had four corps of which VII and VIII Corps would be the focus in Operation Cobra. The VII Corps commander, **Major General J. Lawton Collins**, had commanded an infantry division during the fighting on Guadalcanal where he picked up his nickname, "Lightning Joe." He was one of the few senior US Army commanders to fight in both the Pacific and European theaters, the other being Charles H. Corlett, who commanded the XIX Corps on the left flank. Collins' corps had been responsible for the first major US victory in Normandy, the capture of Cherbourg. Bradley selected VII Corps to carry out the most essential element of the Cobra break-out plan. The VIII Corps commander, **Major General Troy Middleton**, had enlisted in the army in 1910 and had risen to regimental command in World War I. He had served as a divisional commander in Sicily and Italy.

Although the First Army would direct the initial phase of Operation Cobra, plans were well under way to expand the US Army in Normandy once the breakthrough had taken place. Beginning in July the new Third Army began to take shape in the western sector of the American zone. In spite of their problems with **General George Patton**, both Eisenhower and Bradley acknowledged that he was their most aggressive commander and best suited to lead any major mechanized assault. Past sins were forgotten and Patton's Third Army was activated on 1 August 1944. As a result of the expansion Bradley was promoted to command the new 12th Army Group consisting of Patton's Third Army, and the existing First Army, now led by Bradley's deputy, Lieutenant General Courtney L. Hodges.

OPPOSING FORCES

GERMAN FORCES

The Normandy campaign highlighted the continuing de-modernization of the German Army during the later years of the war. This was most striking in the area of air support. The Luftwaffe was never a significant factor in Normandy, in complete contrast to the Allied air forces. Both the British and US air forces learned the lessons from their inadequate performance in Tunisia in 1943, and in Normandy they played a pivotal role both in paralyzing German logistics, and in dominating the battlefield with close air support. This was not only a tactical matter, but one of strategic vision as well. Hitler and the senior leadership did not have any comprehension of how significant air power could be on the modern battlefield. Experienced combat leaders like Kluge and Model were shocked after their arrival in Normandy to see how decisive air power had become as compared to the relatively modest role it played on the Russian front.

Airpower was only the most dramatic example of how far the German army had slipped since 1940. In many other respects such as army motorization, and command-and-control, it was significantly behind the

By the time of Operation Cobra, many of the best German units had been badly worn down. The Panzer Lehr Division would bear the brunt of the Cobra attack, and had lost a quarter of its armor during an ill-fated counter-offensive in mid-July around Le Desert, of which these two knocked-out Panther tanks were victims.

The hedgerow fighting placed a premium on light weapons that could be readily moved. One unusual type of German anti-tank weapon encountered in the Normandy fighting was the 88mm Raketenwerfer 43 *Püppchen* which fired an 88mm rocket to a range of about 700 meters. Weighing about 325 pounds, it fell between the man-portable panzershreck rocket launcher and more conventional anti-tank guns.

western Allies. This became manifest as the battles in Normandy became more fluid. German higher headquarters had a difficult time reacting after the US Army achieved the breakthrough as their lack of a robust radio network prevented senior commanders from contacting their subordinate commands once the land lines and field telephone wires were shattered by bombardment. Movement of troops to counter the breakthrough was made difficult by the lack of motorization, which also affected the ability of German forces to receive adequate logistics support.

The German Seventh Army consisted of units from three German services – the Wehrmacht, the Waffen-SS, and the Luftwaffe. This was a reflection of the "empire building" by Hitler's cronies that plagued the German war effort. The Seventh Army had been involved in combat since June, and most units were in a weakened state as a result. Aside from combat attrition, they were further undermined by a poor supply situation. The US Army Air Force was conducting an interdiction campaign, to isolate the Wehrmacht from their sources of supply. German forces in France had spent the occupation years in relatively static positions, and so were generally not equipped with enough vehicles to move sufficient supplies on their own. They depended instead on the excellent French rail network. However, after the Allied air campaign the railroads were in a shambles. The German army responded by starting river ferry operations, concentrating their bridge rebuilding efforts on a handful of the most vital sites, issuing units with bicycles instead of vehicles for mobility, and requiring divisions to collect their own supplies from dumps further to the rear. While this did improve the transport situation in the eastern area opposite the British sector, Seventh Army continued to suffer from extreme supply problems. Rail traffic over the Loire river remained paralyzed. The key rail bridge at St. Cyr and marshalling yard at Tours were put out of action by air attack on 15 July, and the fuel depot near Châteaubriant was bombed on 16 July. By the time of the Cobra offensive, the Seventh Army was down to about two days' supply of fuel and was low on ammunition as well.

No doubt the most feared weapon in the German arsenal was the 88mm FlaK 36 anti-aircraft gun, widely used in a secondary anti-tank role. However, it was not as common as most GIs seemed to think and nearly any anti-tank was called an "88". The smaller and more versatile 75mm PaK 40 anti-tank gun destroyed far more Allied tanks in Normandy, but most of its victims were credited to the more celebrated "88". This particular gun was captured by US forces on 31 July during Operation Cobra.

German infantry formations in France were of two basic types, static infantry divisions, and regular infantry divisions, sometimes called "attack divisions". The static divisions were used for occupation duty or coastal defense and were manned by over-aged, convalescent, or otherwise second-rate troops. They were often armed with captured weapons, had little organic motor transport, and were often poorly trained. Of the divisions in France these types of units made up about two-thirds of the force. In November 1943 Hitler ordered that steps be taken to improve the quality of the forces in France to meet the expected Allied invasion. There was a steady influx of veterans from the eastern front, but the army in France continued to suffer from a serious shortage of experienced non-commissioned officers due to the tremendous attrition in Russia. Ideological indoctrination was considerably stepped up in late 1943 in an effort to enhance morale and improve unit cohesion and tenacity. By the summer of 1944 there were 12 of the better quality infantry divisions in France, including some excellent paratroop units. These divisions would bear the brunt of the fighting in the bocage country in July and August. Due to manpower shortages the Germans preferred "tooth over tail", deploying as much strength as possible up front in the infantry companies and as little as possible in the service units. While this had some short-term tactical advantages, the unit's logistical and maintenance weaknesses sapped endurance and combat power in prolonged combat.

In spite of their problems, the German commanders made best use of their infantry divisions with proven tactics and dogged determination. German tactics in Normandy reflected the lessons of 1917–18 refined by eastern front experience. The bocage fighting had some similarities to trench fighting in 1918. The Germans held the forward-edge-of-battle weakly. This prevented their main defenses from being smothered by Allied artillery or air power. Since the bocage was so well suited to defense, a thin forward line was usually adequate to pin the American troops. Once it was clear where the main American thrust was focused, additional units could be moved forward to respond. German infantry tactics were generally more successful than American tactics in the bocage. Also based on their World War I experiences, German squad tactics relied on the MG.42 machine gun. This provided a base of fire for the squad, and the squad's actions hinged around the machine gun team. In contrast, the US infantry attempted to gain firepower dominance with their excellent M1 Garand rifles, but this often proved inadequate. The squad's automatic rifle, the BAR, did not have the high rate of fire of the German machine gun and did not play as central a role as the German machine gun teams. A German infantry company had 13 machine guns compared to only two in a US infantry company. The combination of excellent natural defenses and more practical tactics gave the German infantry a decided edge in defensive operations. But German infantry in Normandy did not have the offensive capability to conduct missions any larger than small unit counterattacks.

The weaknesses of the infantry formations led the Germans to place increasing importance on the panzer and panzer grenadier formations to conduct any counterattacks above regimental size. Furthermore, the heavy attrition of infantry in June and July, especially in the Seventh Army sector opposite the Americans, led the commanders to deploy panzer units in the front line. This led to heavy attrition of equipment and personnel and was contrary to doctrine, which favored the use of the panzer units as a mobile reserve to counterattack breakthroughs. Even though German tank production reached new heights in the summer of 1944, tank replacements were shipped to France in miserly amounts due to Hitler's insistence on the creation of the new panzer brigades to reinforce the shattered eastern front. This was further aggravated by the panzer division's limited repair capability and the low durability of German tanks. For example, on 1 July 58 percent of the Panthers and 42 percent of the PzKpfw IV tanks were out of service for maintenance. By late July, attrition, the tanks' declining mechanical condition, and the lack of replacement tanks seriously undermined the combat power of the panzer divisions in Normandy.

If US tankers feared the "88", US infantry hated the "Screaming meemies", their nickname for German Nebelwerfer multiple artillery rocket launchers. The nickname came from the howl that the large rockets made as they descended on their target. This is a 30cm Nebelwerfer 42, which could fire six rockets, each with a 45kg warhead, to a range of about 3.5 miles (6km).

21

Due to Kluge's belief that the main threat came in the British sector, Hausser's Seventh Army was starved of troops. The 2nd Parachute Corps held the zone immediately to the south of St. Lô. It was a relatively small corps with the 3rd Parachute Division to the east, and the battered but stalwart 352nd Division immediately to the south of St. Lô. This configuration was chosen since it was felt that the US Army would attempt to break out of St. Lô to the south-east along the Torigni-sur-Vire road, passing through the paratroopers' sector. The 352nd Division was in fact an amalgamation of no fewer than five divisions shattered in the earlier fighting, and had been fighting since the defense of Omaha beach. The 3rd Parachute Division was in far better shape and the paratroopers' training and morale made them the ideal infantry for the dense bocage country.

The 84th Corps was significantly larger, and covered the remainder of the front from St. Lô to the coast. The formations in the center, opposite VII Corps' breakthrough sector, were based around the Panzer Lehr Division. Although Panzer Lehr had entered Normandy earlier in the summer fully equipped, it had taken heavy losses in men and materiel during the July fighting. By 23 July it had been reduced to 80 tanks of which only 16 Panthers and 15 PzKpfw IV tanks were operational. Under the division's command was a new battalion from the 5th Parachute Division, the battalion-strength Kampfgruppe Heintz from the reserve 275th Division, and the small Kampfgruppe Brosow from the 2nd SS Panzer Division. The combat value of Panzer Lehr

German units in Normandy made extensive use of the Sturmgeschutz, a turretless assault gun based on a panzer chassis. There were about 190 StuG's operational in Normandy at the start of Operation Cobra, of which about a third were in the Seventh Army sector. This is a StuG IV based on the PzKpfw IV chassis, which was less common than the StuG III in Normandy. This particular vehicle served with SS-Panzer Abt. 17 of the 17th SS Panzer Grenadier Division and was knocked out during fighting near Periers shortly before the outbreak of Operation Cobra.

Division was graded as *Kampfwert III*, that is suitable for defensive operations. The Panzer Lehr Division rotated its few remaining tanks in and out of front-line duty, strung out like a "string of pearls" between the dismounted panzer grenadier companies. At the time of the Cobra offensive, it was the Panther regiment which had its tanks deployed forward. The division's SdKfz 251 armored halftracks were of little use in bocage fighting, so most were left in the rear.

To the west, the newly constituted 5th Parachute Division had only recently moved into the sector on 21 July so was in good order even if not combat hardened. In the sector facing the US VIII Corps, the 17th SS Panzergrenadier Division had been decimated by heavy fighting in the British sector earlier in the summer and its combat status was rated at only *Kampfwert IV*. The only substantial armor force in the sector was 2nd SS Panzer Division "Das Reich" west of Periers. The unit was infamous for a string of war crimes during its transit from southern France, the most heinous of which took place at Oradour-sur-Glane. It was the only major unit in Seventh Army still rated at *Kampfwert I*, and had 37 Pzkpfw IV, 41 Panthers and 25 StuG assault guns operational in late July, plus additional tanks on hand but being repaired. The division's mission was to prevent the US Army from seizing the coastal road that led to Avranches, the best north–south road in the Cotentin peninsula. The left wing of the Seventh Army included the 91st Airlanding Division, rated at *Kampfwert II*, and the remnants of the 243rd Division, rated at a miserable *Kampfwert V*. There were two divisions in army reserve, the 353rd Infantry Division rated at *Kampfwert II*, and the 275th Infantry Division. In total, the Seventh Army had about 30,000 troops, significantly more than the 17,000 estimated by the US Army, as well as 357 tanks and assault guns.

The weakness of the German formations facing the Americans was exacerbated by their deployment. Hausser had placed all three of his mechanized formations in the front lines, and had left two under-strength infantry divisions as his reserve. This disposition was a cause of concern for Kluge, who had just finished rectifying a similar situation in the neighboring Panzer Group West sector. By transferring four infantry divisions from the Pas-de-Calais and southern France, he was able to shift five panzer divisions from the front lines in mid-July. Hausser had chosen this unfortunate disposition since he felt that his infantry formations were too weak to hold the line. Kluge advised Hausser to pull both the 2nd SS Panzer Division and Panzer Lehr Division back and substitute the two reserve infantry divisions. Hausser dragged his heels on the matter due to the disruption it would cause in his thinly stretched lines. While waiting for the 363rd Infantry Division to arrive, he limited his readjustments to the dispatch of two companies out of the 2nd SS Panzer Division into the reserve. Kluge did not push Hausser on the issue, as he was convinced that the main Allied effort would occur in the British sector. This assessment seemed to be confirmed when Montgomery launched yet another major tank offensive on 18 July – Operation Goodwood.

The German armed forces were the most backward in tactical air support. The Luftwaffe fighter force had been shattered in the spring 1944 air campaigns while attempting to defend the Reich against American daylight bombing attacks. The attrition rate of fighter pilots was so severe that the Luftwaffe had drastically shortened its training program. As a result the new pilots went into combat with grossly inadequate training, and suffered extremely high casualties. The emphasis on air defense fighters led to a gradual atrophy of the fighter-bomber force. Furthermore, there was a very limited appreciation of airpower among the German army commanders who had spent most of the war years on the eastern front. The Red Air Force was not particularly adept at close air support, and so the level of Allied air activity in France was deeply shocking to eastern front veterans. As one of Rommel's advisors noted, close air support represented a revolution in warfare since it "turned the flank not from the side, but from above."

Hausser's Seventh Army received very little air support for its operations. The Luftwaffe's Luftflotte 3 had three fighter groups in the Rennes–Laval area in late July and had about 350 combat aircraft operational per day. They had a sortie rate of about 450 daylight missions and 250 night missions. In spite of this level of effort, only about 30 to 40 sorties per day actually reached their intended target area due to Allied air superiority. For example, on the Luftwaffe's busiest day, 28 July, only 47 aircraft reached US lines of which 14 were shot down. A higher percentage of night sorties reached Allied lines, but these were ineffective due to poor bombing accuracy at night and the presence of Allied night fighters. Some of the daylight effort was frittered away on secondary missions, for example fighter sweeps to deal with Allied artillery spotting aircraft. The small number of close-support missions that were actually conducted proved largely ineffective since Allied offensives were always accompanied by heightened Allied fighter sweeps. In July some aircraft were fitted with new 210mm rocket launchers to improve the capability of the aircraft to deal with Allied tank breakthroughs. There is little evidence they were ever effective.

The limited capabilities of the Luftwaffe had dire consequences in other respects. It made aerial reconnaissance difficult and often impossible. Strategic photographic reconnaissance by high-altitude Me-410 and Ju-188 aircraft were so hazardous that they could be conducted only at night using flares, and daylight missions by low-altitude Bf-109s provided only fragmentary information. The intelligence situation was so poor that in late July the Luftwaffe dispatched two of its new Ar-234 jet aircraft to France. The jets finally managed to secure comprehensive aerial photos of the Normandy bridgehead area on 2 August, the first since the invasion two months before. While conventional intelligence techniques enabled the Seventh Army to make accurate assessments of the number of US divisions facing them along the front, the lack of aerial reconnaissance made it impossible to determine the strength of the US reserve, especially the new armored divisions being moved into the area for the upcoming offensive.

US FORCES

The First US Army had 11 full-strength infantry and three armored divisions committed to Operation Cobra, and reserve divisions available for later stages of the operation. The disproportionate strength was due in no small measure to the US conviction that the difficult bocage

US armored units introduced two important innovations during Operation Cobra, an improved version of the M4A1 tank with a long 76mm gun, and the Culin Rhino device. The Rhino was a set a prongs made from German beach obstructions to cut through the hedgerows as seen in the demonstration here. The 2nd Armored Division had about three-fifths of their tanks fitted with these devices by the time the offensive started on 25 July.

terrain would necessitate overwhelming superiority to accomplish a breakthrough. The usual rule of thumb was a force-ratio of three attackers for every defender, but in the bocage Bradley wanted a six-to-one ratio. The US Army had taken substantial losses in the bocage fighting, especially in the rifle companies – a total of 36,700 casualties in July prior to Cobra. Replacements were available, but several of the divisions lost many of their experienced small unit commanders, and took very high losses among front-line riflemen.

If the previous month and a half of fighting had been costly, it had also been enormously valuable for battle-hardening the US Army. The bocage fighting had separated the better commanders from the mediocre. The US Army studied the lessons from the bocage fighting and began applying the lessons in the weeks before the start of Operation Cobra. At the infantry squad level it was clear that the Germans had a firepower advantage. The American response was to increase the firepower of the squad where possible by acquiring weapons beyond the official tables of organization, especially automatic weapons like Thompson sub-machine guns, and additional BARs. In addition, the infantry came to rely more heavily on artillery to provide a firepower advantage. It was able to do so due to the sheer amount of artillery available as well as to superior communications. The US Army was better equipped with tactical radios than the Germans, including the SCR-598 "handie-talkie" deployed at platoon level and the SCR-300 FM transceiver deployed at company level. Instead of relying on pre-planned artillery strikes, the infantry formations could call in strikes as they advanced.

The bocage terrain was very ill-suited to armor operations. Tanks attempting to surmount the hedgerows exposed their thin belly armor to enemy anti-tank defenses and were easily knocked out. The narrow passages between the hedgerows were ideally suited to ambushes using the deadly panzerfaust or panzershreck anti-tank rockets. The major roads could be covered by dug-in anti-tank guns, most often the deadly 75mm PaK 40. This compact and potent weapon was the most under-rated weapon of the German arsenal, Allied tank crews mistakenly attributing their losses to the rare 88mm gun. It proved difficult to coordinate tank and infantry actions. The tanks used FM radios while the platoon "handie-talkie" operated in AM. Finally, the performance of the US M4 medium tank proved to be disappointing on the occasions when it encountered German panzers. While the M4 could hold its own against the PzKpfw IV, it was no match for the German Panther. The Panther's thicker frontal armor was invulnerable to the 75mm gun of the M4 at any range. In contrast, the high velocity 75mm gun on the Panther could defeat the M4's armor at any practical combat range. While the M4 could knock out a Panther from the side, the bocage restricted mobility. The US Army's intended tank killer, the M10 3-inch tank destroyer, was an even bigger disappointment as its 3-inch gun could not deal with the Panther and its thinner armor and lack of turret roof armor made it very vulnerable. Tank losses in the bocage fighting had been unexpectedly high, about 30 percent a month instead of the anticipated 7 percent.

A variety of steps were taken to improve the tank situation prior to Cobra. Some units had begun to experiment with methods to break through the hedgerows. A young soldier with the 102nd Cavalry, Sergeant Curtis Culin, proposed using steel beams from the German coastal tank traps to create a set of prongs on the tank's bow. Charging into the hedge the prongs penetrated the mass of roots and allowed the tank to plow through the hedge without exposing its belly. After a few experiments with Culin's "Rhino", First Army locally manufactured 500 of the them. It was considered top secret and reserved for the Cobra operation. Combat engineer troops suggested the use of the new M1 tank dozer, which could also be used to break gaps in the hedgerows. Delivery of dozer tanks was accelerated with an aim to having four in each battalion by the time of the start of Cobra. To help in tank–infantry cooperation, ordnance crews began attaching field telephones to the rear of tanks, connected into the tank's intercom system. This allowed the infantry to communicate directly with the tank crew from the protection of the rear of the tank. While not an ideal solution it proved better than nothing.

Another new piece of equipment to debut during Cobra was a more heavily armed version of the M4 tank, the M4A1 (76mm). This had been developed in 1943 by mating a high-velocity 76mm gun in a new turret to the existing M4, M4A1 and M4A3 tanks. Although available earlier in

1944, there had been considerable resistance in the US Army about fielding the new design prior to the Normandy landings. Some tank officers felt that the gun's one advantage, its better armor penetration, did not outweigh its disadvantages. Unlike the 75mm gun on the Panther, it was not fitted with a muzzle brake and so tended to kick up a great deal of dust, obscuring the target and making a corrected shot difficult. In addition it's high explosive round was inferior to that on the medium-velocity 75mm gun already on the M4. The shock of the Panther tank quelled any further debate over the matter, and both the 2nd and 3rd Armored Divisions each received 51 M4A1 (76mm) tanks in time for Cobra. In the event its performance against the Panther was disappointing.

A more important innovation introduced for Cobra was the so-called "armored column cover". In contrast to the Germans, the US Army had extensive air support. The trick was how best to use it. The First Army had its own air force, the 9th Tactical Air Command, led by Major General Elwood "Pete" Quesada. Unlike the situation today, many of the World War II air force commanders had served in the ground forces before switching to aviation billets, and Quesada was one of these. As a result the tactical air force leaders were very responsive to army concerns. The 9th TAC had 18 fighter, fighter-bomber and reconnaissance groups with about 400 combat aircraft. During the

Troops of the 2nd Armored Division and some other units were issued camouflage battle-dress for Operation Cobra like these armored infantry troops in Pont Brocard. Since camouflage uniforms were far more common amongst German troops, there were a number of instances when the US troops were mistaken for Germans. As a result the camouflage suits were abandoned in August in favor of the ubiquitous field drab.

bocage fighting, the 9th TAC had provided air support in two forms, pre-planned missions and immediate response missions. Pre-planned missions were usually requested a day in advance, and if approved, took place the following day. Immediate missions were requested by air support parties attached to army formations. These requests were sent by radio to the joint combined operations center, and then passed on to the fighter-bomber groups. While a highly effective system in static warfare conditions, the "immediate" missions were not in fact so timely as their name would suggest.

Quesada came up with the idea of dedicating a portion of the P-47 fighter-bomber force to the lead elements of the Cobra spearhead. A total of four-to-eight Thunderbolts would fly along with the lead column, armed with 500-pound bombs. They could perform armed reconnaissance in front of the column, and if the column encountered resistance, the aircraft would be available to attack the German position. Earlier attempts at this tactic had floundered as a result of the incompatibility of tank and aircraft radios, and the difficulties of identifying the targets to the pilots from the ground. To avoid these problems, Quesada arranged to have a limited number of M4 tanks modified to carry SCR-522 VHF radios operated by pilots more familiar with the needs of the Thunderbolt crews. During Operation Cobra, three units, the 366th, 404th, and 368th Fighter Groups provided armored column cover.

The M1 155mm howitzer served in one field artillery battalion in each infantry division. It was also used in non-divisional battalions like this one from VIII Corps supporting the 90th Division on 28 July during Operation Cobra. During the war the US Army remained segregated, and this is one of a number of African-American field artillery battalions that served in France during the war.

Artillery had proven to be the US Army's one main advantage in Normandy. Although the technical performance of the cannon on both sides was similar, the US artillery was fully motorized while much of German artillery was horse-drawn. The US artillery enjoyed substantial advantages in communications and fire control, having a robust radio net essential for mobile operations. The US Army pioneered the fire direction center, which allowed the use of more lethal artillery tactics such as the "serenade" or, as it was officially known, "time-on-target". This delivered the blows of multiple batteries or battalions simultaneously against a single target, giving the enemy troops no time to dive for cover. Ammunition was in short supply at the time of Cobra, but the US forces had far more than the Germans.

Another critical factor in Operation Cobra was the Allied advantage in intelligence. Due to Allied air superiority, regular photo reconnaissance could be undertaken to monitor German activity. The Allies continued to read German radio traffic due to success in breaking the Enigma coding system. This provided a considerable amount of detail about the harried state of the German Seventh Army, even daily strength reports. These advantages were further reinforced by the support of the French resistance, which could often provide timely information about German troop movements and locations.

American tactics for Cobra differed from the tactics used by the British and Canadian armies in the Caen area. While most of the assaults in this sector were spearheaded by armored divisions due to British shortages of infantry, this was contrary to US tactical doctrine. The US pattern was to use infantry divisions, backed by separate tank and tank destroyer battalions, to achieve the initial the breakthrough. Only after the breakthrough was accomplished would the armored divisions be committed.

Heavy firepower was provided by non-divisional M1 8in. howitzer units like the 105th Field Artillery Battalion seen here supporting the First Army near Carentilly on 31 July 1944. In contrast to the Wehrmacht, which depended heavily on horse-drawn artillery, US artillery was heavily mechanized like this M4 18-ton high speed tractor.

Collins had the pick of the divisions for the VII Corps assault. For the initial phase of the operation he selected the 9th and 30th Infantry Divisions. The 9th Division, a veteran unit from North Africa and Sicily, had taken over 3,500 casualties in the bocage fighting and was far from fresh. The 30th "Old Hickory" Division was commanded by Major General Leland "Hollywood" Hobbs, a skilled and flamboyant commander with a bad temper. Like the 9th Division, the 30th had taken heavy casualties in the bocage fighting, but had also proven itself and developed critical battle experience. In the wings to assist in exploiting the breakthrough was the 1st Infantry Division, the "Big Red One", commanded by Major General Clarence Huebner, who had a distinguished career with the unit dating back to World War I.

To conduct the exploitation phase, Collins' corps had two of the army's three heavy armored divisions, the 2nd and 3rd Armored Divisions. These maintained the earlier regimental structure rather than the 1943 battalion structure of the remaining armored divisions. The 2nd Armored Division had seen combat in North Africa and Sicily. The 3rd Armored's first campaign was in Normandy, and it had taken significant losses in the fighting in the bocage in July. Both divisions had been brought up to full strength for the offensive. In total the 2nd Armored had 236 M4 medium and 158 M5A1 light tanks on hand at the beginning of Cobra while the 3rd had 241 M4 medium and 158 M5A1 light tanks. The 4th Armored Division saw its combat debut during Cobra, and started the fighting with 165 M4 medium tanks and 83 M5A1 light tanks. It was configured under the new 1943 table of organization with fewer tanks but more armored infantry and artillery. Besides these three armored divisions, First Army had a total of 13 separate tank battalions attached to the infantry divisions. In total US First Army had 1,269 M4 medium tanks and 694 M5A1 light tanks at the start of Operation Cobra, roughly a ten-to-one advantage over its German opponents in medium tanks. In addition, there were nine self-propelled and five towed tank destroyer battalions attached to the divisions, adding a further 288 M10 3in. GMC and 36 M18 76mm GMC to the total number of armored vehicles in First Army service.

Ultimately the defeat of the German army in Normandy depended in large measure on the performance of the troops and commanders. The US Army, which had demonstrated lackluster performance in Tunisia and Italy, had undergone a steady transformation through late 1943 and 1944. These improvements gave it the combat power to carry out sustained offensive operations, a capability which the Wehrmacht was losing by 1944.

ORDER OF BATTLE, ST. LÔ SECTOR, 24 JULY 1944

US FORCES

US First Army Group — **General Omar N. Bradley**

VIII Corps — **MajGen Troy H. Middleton**
79th Infantry Division — MajGen Ira T. Wyche
8th Infantry Division — MajGen Donald A. Stroh
90th Infantry Division — MajGen Eugene M. Landrum
4th Armored Division — MajGen John S. Wood
83rd Infantry Division — MajGen Robert C. Macon

VII Corps — **MajGen J. Lawton Collins**
9th Infantry Division — MajGen Manton S. Eddy
30th Infantry Division — MajGen Leland S. Hobbs
1st Infantry Division — MajGen Clarence R. Huebner
4th Infantry Division — MajGen Raymond O. Barton
2nd Armored Division — MajGen Edward H. Brooks
3rd Armored Division — MajGen Leroy H. Watson

XIX Corps — **MajGen Charles H. Corlett**
35th Infantry Division — MajGen Paul W. Baade

V Corps — **MajGen Leonard T. Gerow**
2nd Infantry Division — MajGen Walter M. Robertson
5th Infantry Division — MajGen Stafford L. Irwin

GERMAN FORCES

German Seventh Army — **Oberstgruppenführer SS Paul Hausser**

84th Corps — **General der Infanterie Dietrich von Choltitz**
243rd Infantry Division — Generalmajor Berhard Klosterkemper (Col Kemper)*

91st Air Landing Division — Generalleutnant Eugen König (Col Bissig)
2nd SS Panzer Division "Das Reich" — Standartenführer Christian Tychsen
17th SS Panzer Grenadier Division "Götz von Berlichingen" — Brigadeführer Otto Baum

5th Parachute Division — Generalmajor Gustav Wilke
Panzer Lehr Division — Generalleutnant Fritz Bayerlein
353rd Infantry Division — Generalleutnant Erich Müller
275th Division — Generalleutnant Hans Schmidt

2nd Parachute Corps — **General der Fallschirmtruppen Eugen Meindl**
352nd Infantry Division — Generalleutnant Dietrich Kraiss
3rd Parachute Division — Generalmajor Richard Schimpf

*Nominal commander of division listed; actual commander
of divisional remnants listed in parentheses where applicable.

OPPOSING PLANS

In late June, the SHAEF staff had developed a plan called "Lucky Strike", which examined the opportunities should the German defensive line in Normandy crack. It was becoming increasingly evident from intelligence that the Germans had committed much of their reserves and that they lacked any defense in depth, especially in the American sector. Operation Cobra was intended to exploit these weaknesses and take advantage of the growing strength of US Army units in the beachhead. Cobra was part of a larger scheme to liberate France, including a landing operation in southern France. Senior US commanders in World War II have been frequently faulted for their lack of operational vision. Yet their continued insistence on a second invasion through southern France, in spite of Churchill's dogged resistance, suggests otherwise. It was not the success of Operation Cobra alone which would force German withdrawal from France. The landings near Marseilles, codenamed Dragoon, would lead to the precipitous rout of German troops from the Atlantic and Mediterranean coasts. The threat of a southern landing convinced Hitler to maintain significant forces along the Mediterranean, including the 11th Panzer Division, the only armored force not committed to Normandy by early August.

After winning Eisenhower's approval, Bradley presented the Cobra plan to the corps commanders and senior staff at his Omaha beach

To improve the cross-country mobility of the tank units, they were fitted with Rhino prongs on the bow to cut through the hedgerows like this M4 on the right. The vehicle to the left is an M10 3in. gun motor carriage, the standard equipment in US tank destroyer battalions at the time.

Although not as widely touted as the Culin Rhino, many tank units found that the M1 dozer blade was a more effective method to cut through hedgerows. This is an early experiment using a dozer to push through the bocage conducted by First Army engineers on 13 July before the start of Cobra.

headquarters on 12 July. After discussion many changes were introduced, especially by the lead corps commander "Lightning Joe" Collins. The original plan called for the operation to start on 18 July, but this proved premature as the 9th and 30th Division did not capture the Periers–St. Lô road jump-off point until 20 July, and the vital city of St. Lô was not firmly in US hands until 19 July. In addition a considerable portion of the strategic bomber force needed for the preliminary carpet-bombing effort was committed to supporting Montgomery's Operation Goodwood.

The Cobra plan was finalized in field orders on 20 July. Cobra took on added importance when Operation Goodwood failed to achieve a breakthrough in the British sector. At a cost of more than a third of the total British tank strength in theater, the offensive had captured only 32 square miles of territory and made a penetration barely six miles deep. Despite these disappointing results Goodwood had vital consequences for Operation Cobra since it reinforced the German belief that the main Allied thrust would come in the British sector. As a result Hausser's Seventh Army remained starved of new panzer forces, even though there were ample signs that the US Army was planning a major effort near St. Lô.

Cobra was to start with a carpet-bombing of the area immediately in front of Collins' VII Corps. The attitude of the leadership of the 8th Air Force to providing close air support with heavy bombers was unenthusiastic at best. The airmen began to grumble about being called upon to save the ground forces every time they ran into "a spot of

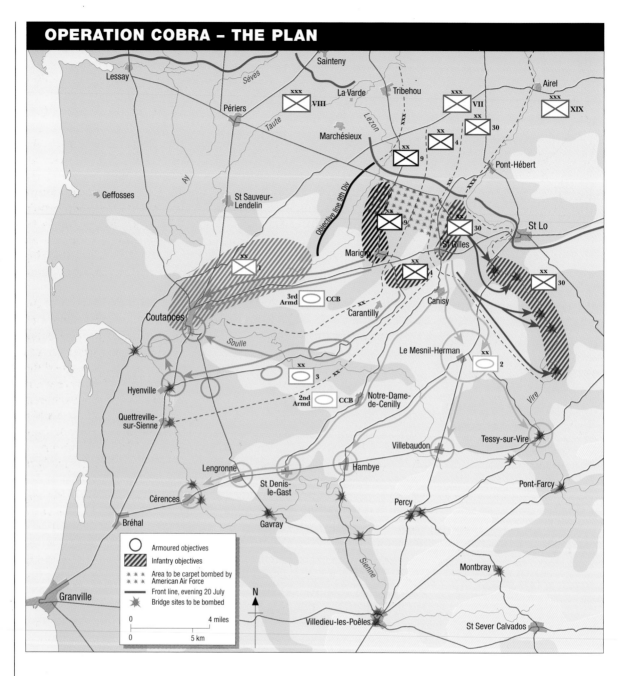

Legend:

- ○ Armoured objectives
- ▨ Infantry objectives
- ⁂ Area to be carpet bombed by American Air Force
- ── Front line, evening 20 July
- ✶ Bridge sites to be bombed

N

0 ——————— 4 miles
0 ——————— 5 km

trouble". The ideology of the 8th Air Force was strategic bombing of German industrial centers, and they preferred to let the 9th TAC handle the close-air support. Past experience had not been encouraging. The British had preceded both Operations Charnwood and Goodwood with a carpet-bombing and neither attack had succeeded. Bradley did not abandon the idea as a result of these experiences, but did learn valuable lessons. During Operation Charnwood the heavy bombs used created large craters that slowed the advance of the tanks. Bradley wanted the bombers to use 100lb bombs to minimize cratering. In addition Bradley proposed to launch the ground offensive in the immediate aftermath of the bombing, with the US troops only 800 yards from the edge of the

One of the lessons from the bocage fighting was the need for better tank–infantry cooperation. A simple but effective innovation introduced before Cobra was the installation of a telephone mounted in a .30cal ammunition box on the rear of the tank, wired to the tank's internal intercom system. This allowed accompanying infantry to talk to the tank crew and help coordinate their actions.

bomb zone. To minimize the possibilities of casualties Bradley wanted the bombers to fly parallel to the front line. To reduce the chances for mistakes, Bradley insisted that US forces secure the Perier–St. Lô road area prior to Cobra, since the road would provide a natural and visible boundary for the northern edge of the bomb zone.

The bomber commanders were not happy about the proposals, arguing that the attack should be perpendicular to the front line so that the bombers did not have to run a gauntlet of German flak. Aware of the lack of precision inherent in carpet-bombing with heavy bombers, they were aghast at the idea that friendly troops would be only 800 yards from the edge of the bomb zone, and would have preferred a separation of three miles. In the end a compromise was reached and the troops would pull back 1,200 yards. The strip closest to friendly forces would be attacked by low-altitude fighter-bombers. A final meeting between the air and ground commanders was held on 19 July, with both sides thinking that they had reached a common agreement. As time would tell there were still issues that had not been adequately clarified.

Bradley's intentions in Cobra were to push the US forces out of the bocage and into the uplands further south where they could maneuver. The immediate objective of VII Corps was to penetrate beyond the German main line of resistance, and once this occurred to sweep west to seize the town of Coutances. The 30th Infantry Division was assigned the task of swinging east to seize a line along the Vire river to prevent the Germans from cutting off the breakthrough by an attack from the east. While VII Corps plunged forward, the other corps would conduct limited operations in their own sectors to prevent German units from sending reinforcements to the breakthrough sector. The ultimate aim of the initial phase of the operation was to position the US Army ready to plunge into Brittany to seize the ports.

A deeper breakout would necessitate additional forces and Bradley had these on hand by the end of the month in the form of Patton's Third Army. This aspect of the plans was a more tightly held secret, and even the corps commanders had not been briefed on Patton's role. However, Bradley had told Collins, without providing any details, that "If this thing goes as it should, we should be in Avranches in a week." Avranches was the gateway into Brittany, and Bradley clearly wanted a breakout, not merely a breakthrough.

The German army had no strategic plan beyond Hitler's insistence that the Normandy bridgehead be contained. The heavy attrition of German infantry units in the June and July fighting led to continual requests to shift units from less active fronts to Normandy. While enough troops were provided to plug gaps in the line, there were never enough reinforcements to allow Kluge to build up adequate reserves. Furthermore, the Allies' campaign against the French rail and road systems made it equally impossible to shift forces rapidly from other sectors in the event of a breakthrough. German units still in the Fifteenth Army in the Pas de Calais would have to travel by rail via Paris, but this rail line was too badly damaged to allow this. Hitler did not consent to the creation of a secondary defense line, the so-called "Kitzinger" line, until late August, by which time it was too late.

Kluge evidently was not expecting any major developments in the St. Lô sector, as he was away from his headquarters in the Caen sector

Kluge confers with his staff in the field. During the days preceding Operation Cobra Kluge was primarily concerned with the threat posed by British forces in the sector around Caen, and paid far less attention to the American sector, which he believed could be more easily contained. (MHI)

inspecting troops when Cobra struck. Although Hausser later stated that the premature 24 July bombing of the Periers–St. Lô road convinced him a major attack was coming, he did not have a clear impression of American intentions. He expected the main American blow to emanate out of the St. Lô area south-east towards the Vire river, since the terrain west of the city was so poorly suited to a major attack. However his dispositions placed his most powerful strike force, the 2nd SS Panzer Division, closer to the coast to cover the main north–south road leading into Brittany.

The chief of staff of OB West, General Günther Blumentritt later recalled: "Although most of the German high command regarded the British as more dangerous, which resulted in the concentration of more troops and good panzer divisions near Caen, there was a decided shift in opinion as the battles in Normandy progressed. Panzer Lehr Division was actually shifted to the American front, and there is no doubt that other divisions would have been shifted to oppose the Americans had they not been tied down by continued British pressure and the overall lack of reserves. We recognized all along that Montgomery was more methodical than most American commanders, and we admired the quick, deft stroke which cut the Cherbourg peninsula and the speedy regrouping of American forces following the fall of Cherbourg itself." By the time that the German high command began to reassess their views about the Allied threat, it was too late.

OPERATION COBRA

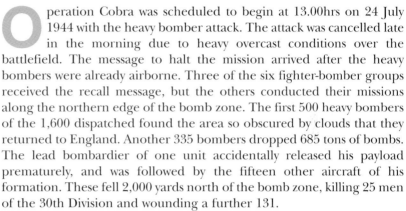

peration Cobra was scheduled to begin at 13.00hrs on 24 July 1944 with the heavy bomber attack. The attack was cancelled late in the morning due to heavy overcast conditions over the battlefield. The message to halt the mission arrived after the heavy bombers were already airborne. Three of the six fighter-bomber groups received the recall message, but the others conducted their missions along the northern edge of the bomb zone. The first 500 heavy bombers of the 1,600 dispatched found the area so obscured by clouds that they returned to England. Another 335 bombers dropped 685 tons of bombs. The lead bombardier of one unit accidentally released his payload prematurely, and was followed by the fifteen other aircraft of his formation. These fell 2,000 yards north of the bomb zone, killing 25 men of the 30th Division and wounding a further 131.

The friendly casualties from the bombing caused a major dust-up between Bradley's staff and the air commanders. Bradley was under the impression that the air force commanders would stage the bombardment parallel to the Periers–St. Lô highway not perpendicular to minimize the chance of casualties. The air force disagreed, fearing heavy losses to flak since the bombers would be flying unusually low – only 15,000 feet. Bradley was also concerned that the aborted bombing mission would alert the Germans to the planned offensive and lose the element of surprise. In fact it had little impact on Hausser's plans since he had so few resources anyway. Weather forecasts for the following day seemed better and Bradley ordered the air attack to take place on 25 July.

Panzer Lehr Division had weathered the first air attack with modest casualties – about 350 men and 10 armored vehicles. The division's commander, Fritz Bayerlein, was convinced that his forces had repulsed a major US attack. In anticipation of more fighting, he ordered his forward outpost line from positions north of the Periers–St. Lô highway to the south where they would be less vulnerable to US artillery. This placed them immediately inside the most intense sector of the bomb zone the next day. The aborted 24 July attack confused German higher headquarters. While Hausser reiterated his concern that the Americans planned a significant action in his sector, he did not seem unduly alarmed in a conversation with Kluge. As a result Kluge continued his inspection of Panzer Group West on 25 July.

Operation Cobra started with a devastating carpet–bombing of a section along the D900 Periers-St. Lô road by 1,495 B-17 and B-24 heavy bombers. This is one of the few known photos of the mission from Patton's personal collection. The view looks to the west, and the bomb impacts in the lower left of the photo are covering the area around Chapelle-en-Juger near the intersections of Routes D900 and D972. A B-24 Liberator bomber appears at the top of the photo. (Patton Museum)

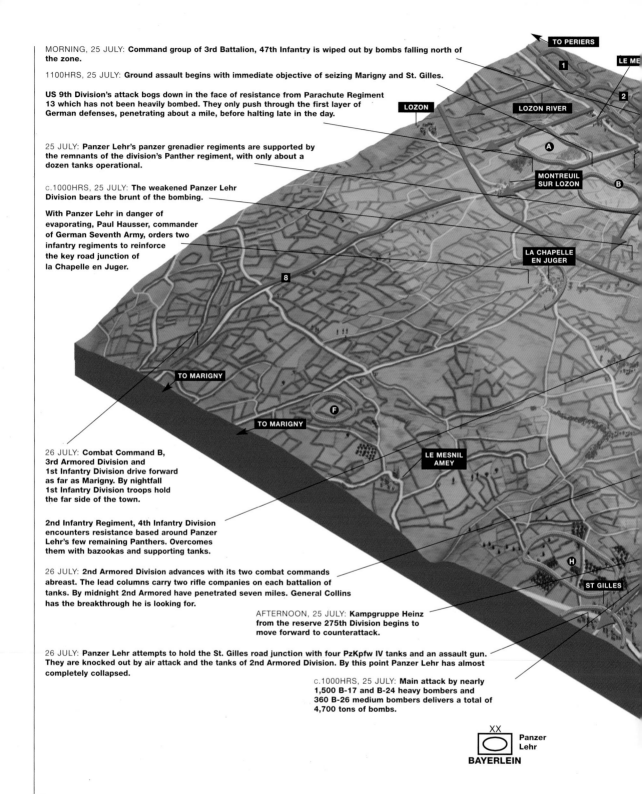

MORNING, 25 JULY: **Command group of 3rd Battalion, 47th Infantry is wiped out by bombs falling north of the zone.**

1100HRS, 25 JULY: **Ground assault begins with immediate objective of seizing Marigny and St. Gilles.**

US 9th Division's attack bogs down in the face of resistance from Parachute Regiment 13 which has not been heavily bombed. They only push through the first layer of German defenses, penetrating about a mile, before halting late in the day.

25 JULY: **Panzer Lehr's panzer grenadier regiments are supported by the remnants of the division's Panther regiment, with only about a dozen tanks operational.**

c.1000HRS, 25 JULY: **The weakened Panzer Lehr Division bears the brunt of the bombing.**

With Panzer Lehr in danger of evaporating, Paul Hausser, commander of German Seventh Army, orders two infantry regiments to reinforce the key road junction of la Chapelle en Juger.

26 JULY: **Combat Command B, 3rd Armored Division and 1st Infantry Division drive forward as far as Marigny. By nightfall 1st Infantry Division troops hold the far side of the town.**

2nd Infantry Regiment, 4th Infantry Division encounters resistance based around Panzer Lehr's few remaining Panthers. Overcomes them with bazookas and supporting tanks.

26 JULY: **2nd Armored Division advances with its two combat commands abreast. The lead columns carry two rifle companies on each battalion of tanks. By midnight 2nd Armored have penetrated seven miles. General Collins has the breakthrough he is looking for.**

AFTERNOON, 25 JULY: **Kampgruppe Heinz from the reserve 275th Division begins to move forward to counterattack.**

26 JULY: **Panzer Lehr attempts to hold the St. Gilles road junction with four PzKpfw IV tanks and an assault gun. They are knocked out by air attack and the tanks of 2nd Armored Division. By this point Panzer Lehr has almost completely collapsed.**

c.1000HRS, 25 JULY: **Main attack by nearly 1,500 B-17 and B-24 heavy bombers and 360 B-26 medium bombers delivers a total of 4,700 tons of bombs.**

TO PERIERS

LE ME

1

2

LOZON

LOZON RIVER

A

MONTREUIL
SUR LOZON

B

LA CHAPELLE
EN JUGER

8

TO MARIGNY

TO MARIGNY

F

LE MESNIL
AMEY

H

ST GILLES

XX
Panzer
Lehr
BAYERLEIN

CARPET BOMBING OF PANZER LEHR DIVISION

25–26 July 1944, viewed from the south east, showing the initial devastating bombing attacks, the US attacks of 25 July and the breakthrough on 26 July

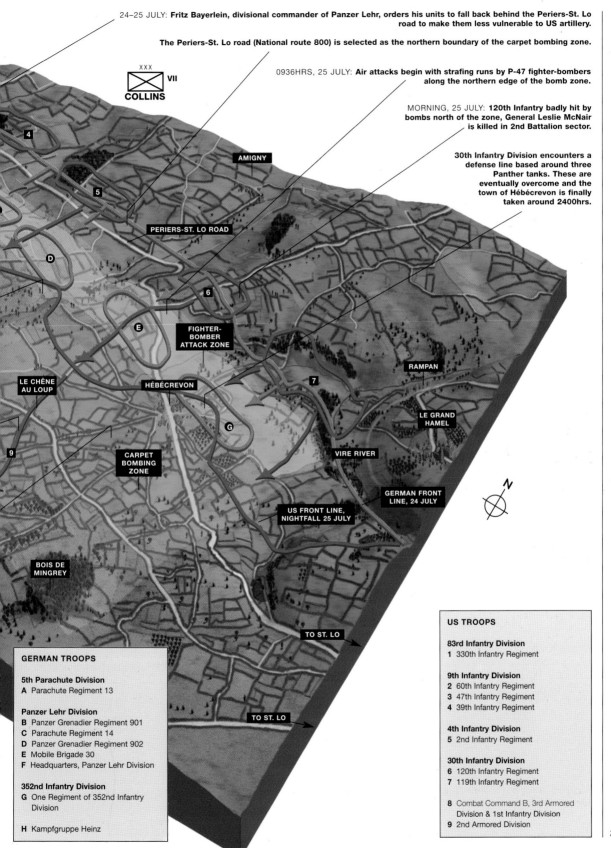

24–25 JULY: Fritz Bayerlein, divisional commander of Panzer Lehr, orders his units to fall back behind the Periers-St. Lo road to make them less vulnerable to US artillery.

The Periers-St. Lo road (National route 800) is selected as the northern boundary of the carpet bombing zone.

0936HRS, 25 JULY: Air attacks begin with strafing runs by P-47 fighter-bombers along the northern edge of the bomb zone.

MORNING, 25 JULY: 120th Infantry badly hit by bombs north of the zone, General Leslie McNair is killed in 2nd Battalion sector.

30th Infantry Division encounters a defense line based around three Panther tanks. These are eventually overcome and the town of Hébécrevon is finally taken around 2400hrs.

XXX
VII
COLLINS

4

AMIGNY

5

PERIERS-ST. LO ROAD

D

6

E

FIGHTER-BOMBER ATTACK ZONE

RAMPAN

LE CHÊNE AU LOUP

HÉBÉCREVON

7

LE GRAND HAMEL

G

9

CARPET BOMBING ZONE

VIRE RIVER

US FRONT LINE, NIGHTFALL 25 JULY

GERMAN FRONT LINE, 24 JULY

N

BOIS DE MINGREY

TO ST. LO

TO ST. LO

GERMAN TROOPS

5th Parachute Division
A Parachute Regiment 13

Panzer Lehr Division
B Panzer Grenadier Regiment 901
C Parachute Regiment 14
D Panzer Grenadier Regiment 902
E Mobile Brigade 30
F Headquarters, Panzer Lehr Division

352nd Infantry Division
G One Regiment of 352nd Infantry Division

H Kampfgruppe Heinz

US TROOPS

83rd Infantry Division
1 330th Infantry Regiment

9th Infantry Division
2 60th Infantry Regiment
3 47th Infantry Regiment
4 39th Infantry Regiment

4th Infantry Division
5 2nd Infantry Regiment

30th Infantry Division
6 120th Infantry Regiment
7 119th Infantry Regiment

8 Combat Command B, 3rd Armored Division & 1st Infantry Division
9 2nd Armored Division

The air attack on 25 July started at 09.36 with strafing runs by P-47 fighter-bombers along the northern edge of the bomb zone. They were followed by 1,495 B-17s and B-24 heavy bombers in several waves, dropping 3,370 tons of bombs into an area 7,000 yards long and 2,500 yards wide. A further 380 B-26 medium bombers completed the attack, bringing the grand total to 4,700 tons of bombs. Anti-aircraft fire was light, and a number of anti-aircraft guns were destroyed by US artillery counter-fire.

The effect on the German defenses was devastating. Of the 3,600 troops under Panzer Lehr Division's immediate control, about 1,000 were killed in the bombing attack, and at least as many wounded or severely dazed. The German communications network, which depended heavily on field telephones, was completely disrupted. The only combat effective unit available to the division by late morning was Kampfgruppe Heintz, which was stationed to the south-east outside the bomb zone. But the bombing coverage was patchy. The damage was worse in the center of the bomb zone where the heavy bombers had struck, while some defensive positions closer to the American lines – including about half the tanks – had gone unscathed.

BELOW **Troops of the 47th Infantry, 9th Division move through a breach in the hedgerow created by a dozer tank on 25 July. The 9th Division had suffered significant casualties in the preceding weeks and lacked tank support during the initial breakthrough attempt.**

RIGHT **A day after the initial
attack, GIs inspect some of the
equipment abandoned by the
Panzer Lehr Division along the
Periers–St. Lô road after
the carpet-bombing. In the
foreground is a SdKfz 251/7
armored half-track fitted with
engineer bridging equipment,
with a disabled Panther Ausf. A
behind it. A half-dozen Panthers
survived the initial bombing but
were quickly overwhelmed by
the ensuing infantry attack.**

The 25 July air attack repeated the problems of the previous day, with bombs again falling short into American lines, killing 111 and wounding 490 soldiers. Among them was Lieutenant General Lesley McNair, head of Army Ground Forces, the highest ranking US officer to die in the war. The casualties were especially severe in the forward assault companies, causing significant problems in launching the initial attacks.

In spite of the bombing errors, the ground attack began at 11.00 with the immediate objective of seizing Marigny and St. Gilles about three miles from the start line. The western portion of the attack bogged down quickly as the defensive positions of Parachute Regiment 13 of 5th Parachute Division had not been heavily bombed. Eddy's 9th Division was surprised to find continued German resistance, and only managed to push through the first layer of the German defenses before halting late in the day. A single regiment from the 4th Division encountered a defensive position based around the few remaining Panther tanks of Panzer Lehr Division, but overcame them with bazookas and supporting tanks. Likewise, the 30th Division encountered a defense line based around three Panther tanks, which was eventually overcome. The town of Hébécrevon was finally taken at midnight.

Overall, the first day's attack had been disappointing. Instead of gaining three miles, Collins' VII Corps had only penetrated about a mile. The option was to continue the infantry attack for the next few days in hopes of securing a clean penetration, or act more boldly and commit the mechanized forces the next day. Collins decided on the bolder option. This was based on his assessment that the German defenses were in a shambles. Previously when US forces in Normandy advanced as far as a mile into German positions, they would inevitably be met with fierce, coordinated counterattacks. Instead there was very little evidence of any coordinated response. Collins also realized that too little force had been used in some sectors, notably the tired 9th Division which had no armor support. This would be rectified the next day. The main problem of deploying armor at this stage was congestion on such a narrow front.

By the end of the day Bayerlein reported to Hausser that he had no infantry left and that his division was on the verge of evaporating. Two

THE CARPET-BOMBING ZONE, 25 JULY 1944

Panzer Lehr Division had its 16 operational Panthers "strung like a necklace of pearls" through its forward edge of battle on the morning of 25 July when Operation Cobra struck. Most of the tanks were caught in the initial bomber attack, and were disabled. As often as not, the near misses on the tanks ripped off tracks, killed the crews, or otherwise disabled the tanks. Few tanks suffered the direct hits needed to put them completely out of action. But in the chaos of the attacks, there was neither the time nor resources to repair damaged vehicles. This battlescene shows two disabled Panther tanks moments after the air attack with the injured crews being assisted by divisional medics and other panzer crews. In spite of the intensity of the bomber attack, several Panther tanks remained in action until knocked out during the ensuing infantry assault. (Tony Bryan)

infantry regiments from the reserve were ordered forward to reinforce the defenses at the key road junction at Chapelle-en-Juger, and Hausser committed his modest panzer reserves, a couple of companies of the 2nd SS Panzer Division. Hausser's failure to build up an adequate reserve was now plainly obvious, as was Kluge's failure to address the deficiencies. On learning of the numerous penetrations of the line, Kluge placed an urgent request to the high command for transfer of the 9th Panzer Division from southern France. It would take ten days to move it to the Cotentin area due to Allied air activity. The immediate focus was on plugging the breach.

Collins' exploitation force consisted of the 2nd Armored Division to the east, and the 1st Infantry Division reinforced by Combat Command B (CCB) of the 3rd Armored Division in the west. CCB/3rd Armored led the attack towards Marigny. One of the main problems was traffic congestion and the poor state of the bombed roads. Passing an armored formation and an infantry regiment down narrow country roads, already occupied by the 9th Division, proved difficult. The new dozer tanks proved to be a big help. The armored attacks on 26 July were preceded by 200 sorties by P-47 fighter-bombers against the two key towns of Marigny and St. Gilles. The air attacks inflicted serious losses on

A column from the 33rd Armored Regt., 3rd Armored Division prepare to move forward from the village of Montreuil-sur-Lozon on 26 July. The CCB of the 3rd Armored Division was committed that day to support the attack of the 1st Infantry Division. The vehicle at the head of the column is a M8 75mm howitzer motor carriage, a variant of the M5A1 light tank used as an assault gun in light tank and cavalry units.

regiments of the 353rd Division that Hausser had sent to counterattack. By late afternoon, the CCB/3rd Armored Div. was on the outskirts of Marigny where it was counterattacked by two companies from 2nd SS Panzer Division and the remnants of a regiment from 353rd Division. The attack halted for the night with the 1st Division infantry holding the other side of Marigny.

The eastern spearhead by the 2nd Armored Division moved much more rapidly, with its two combat commands abreast. In order to speed the advance the lead tank columns carried two rifle companies on each battalion of tanks – about eight GI's per tank. Panzer Lehr Division attempted to defend the road junction at St. Gilles with four PzKpfw IV tanks and an assault gun, but two of the tanks were knocked out by air attack and the remainder by the tank column. By midnight, the 2nd Armored Division had penetrated seven miles for the loss of three tanks, due in large measure to the 30th Division's earlier efforts and the almost total collapse of the Panzer Lehr Division. By late afternoon, Collins was convinced that the penetration had been made and that German defenses were crumbling. He ordered the attack to continue through the night, with an emphasis on speed over caution.

Collins next decision was whether to proceed with the planned "right hook" towards Coutances, the aim of which was to bag the western elements of the German Seventh Army. In spite of not yet holding the road junction at Marigny, Collins ordered the attack anyway, with a regiment of the 1st Infantry Division assigned to take the town. Early on the morning of 27 July, CCB/3rd Armored Division sent three task forces, each consisting of a company of M4 tanks and a company of armored infantry in M3 half-tracks, down the Coutances road. One of the groups ran into an ambush by a Panther tank from 2nd SS Panzer Division commanded by Ernst Barkmann. Three M4 tanks were quickly knocked out, but Barkmann's Panther was damaged by tank fire and supporting air cover and withdrew. The incident was wildly exaggerated by German propaganda, and has acquired mythic status in recent accounts of the Normandy campaign in spite of its insignificance. The CCB/3rd Armored Division task forces advanced four miles in four hours, and by mid-afternoon reached its objective at Camprond. The 2nd Armored Division continued its advance in spectacular fashion, with CCA exploiting the weakness along the German corps boundary, and plunging further south beyond Pont Brocard. Equally important the US

THE BREAKTHROUGH

Although the 2nd Armored Division had fitted Culin hedgerow cutters to nearly three-quarters of the tanks in the assault waves, they were not as widely used as the legend would suggest. Once the infantry had penetrated the shattered defenses of the Panzer Lehr Division, the 2nd Armored Division rapidly exploited gaps in German defenses. When possible, the tank units preferred to use country roads for speed. The armored column cover provided by P-47 Thunderbolts of the 9th TAC was essential in such tactics since the fighter-bombers could provide armed reconnaissance in front of the advance. If German defenses were encountered, they could be bombed and strafed before the tanks arrived. The tanks here are the M4 medium tank with 75mm gun, the most common type in service in July even though about 100 of the newer type with 76mm gun had arrived for the offensive. The First US Army adopted a camouflage pattern of black over olive drab during the Normandy fighting, and the prominent white Allied star insignia were usually painted out for fear of acting as a prominent target for German anti-tank gunners. (Tony Bryan)

VIII Corps had begun its offensive in the western sector, pushing south of the Periers road and taking the town of Periers against relatively light resistance.

Hausser quickly appreciated that the Americans were trying to tie down the 84th Corps and then envelope it from behind by seizing Coutances. He began steps to withdraw the exposed 84th Corps south to the Geffosses–St.Saveur–Lendelin road. Permission to withdraw was delayed, as Kluge was still in the Caen sector until late in the afternoon of 27 July but he was finally reached. However, neither Kluge nor Hausser had any idea of how calamitous the situation was in the Panzer Lehr sector. In addition to the 9th Panzer Division, Kluge received Hitler's permission to transfer three infantry divisions from the Pas de Calais.

The attacks on 28 July 1944 undermined the orderly German withdrawal. With the 84th Corps retreating towards Coutances, Middleton's VIII Corps unleashed its two fresh spearheads, the 4th and 6th Armored Divisions. By nightfall the 4th Armored Division was at the doorsteps of Coutances after facing little opposition. In the center Collins released CCA of 3rd Armored Division, which rushed through the Marigny–St. Gilles gap to Cerisy-la-Salle. The most impressive performance was again by the 2nd Armored Division. It's CCB raced down the highway past St. Denis-le-Gast, cutting the road south out of Coutances near Lengronne and Cambry. It's CCA continued its mission of forming an eastern shield for the Cobra operation, reaching Villebaudon.

THE DEATH RIDE OF DAS REICH

By late afternoon on 28 July it was becoming apparent to Dietrich von Choltitz, the 84th Corps commander, that his forces were on the verge of being encircled. American patrols were penetrating deep behind German lines, often in the most unexpected of locations. The 2nd SS Panzer Division commander was killed by a US patrol near his command post, and Hausser himself was almost captured by another US patrol. Command of the 2nd SS Panzer Division and 17th SS Panzer Grenadier

The CCA, 2nd Armored Division reached the road junction at Canisy by the late afternoon of 26 July after part of the town had been set ablaze by an air attack. There was little resistance from the shattered Panzer Lehr Division. This is an M8 armored car of the division's 82nd Recon Bn.

Although the Panther battalion of Panzer Lehr Division was caught in the initial Cobra bombing attack, the PzKpfw IV battalion was recuperating in the rear. Nevertheless, the battalion lost most of its tanks like this one during skirmishes with the 2nd Armored Division in the ensuing days. Of the 70 in service at the beginning of July it had only 15 PzKpfw IV left by 1 August.

Division fell to Lieutenant Colonel Otto Baum. He discussed withdrawing the remnants of the units southward along the coast road towards Brehal, where they could avoid the westward-moving US forces, and Choltitz agreed. Hausser had other ideas and decided that it would be better for the 84th Corps to withdraw to the south-east, towards Percy. His rationale was that this force would be in place to support Kluge's planned counterattacks with new units from the Vire river aimed at stopping the US penetration. Choltitz protested strongly, arguing that this would denude the coastal area of major forces, allowing the Americans to plunge south along the coast, and envelop the corps from the west as well. Furthermore, it would force the corps to run the gauntlet of the US divisions now starting to move westward to the coast. Hausser told him to follow orders, and notified Kluge of his plans. Kluge was apoplectic about Hausser's plans. Lacking radio contact, he sent a courier to Hausser insisting that the plans be cancelled and the retreat directed south to Brehal as Choltitz had suggested. By the time that Hausser passed on the orders to Choltitz around midnight, the damage had been done as Choltitz no longer had any lines of communication with the retreating units. The bulk of these forces were located around Roncey and Montpinchon, and began to move towards Percy in the early morning hours.

Collins and the other American commanders expected that the Germans would probably try to break out of the encirclement that evening, and warned their forward patrols. The thinly stretched CCB of 2nd Armored Division was reinforced by the divisional reserve. One German column of about 30 tanks and armored vehicles, led by a Hummel 150mm self-propelled gun, attempted to drive through the crossroads south-west of Notre-Dame-de-Cenilly before dawn. The position was held by a company of armored infantry and some M4 tanks of the 2nd Armored Division. A close-range melee ensued, and when dawn came the Americans still held the crossroads. Along the same road, another column of about 15 PzKpfw IV tanks from the 2nd SS Panzer Division supported by about 200 paratroopers of the 6th Parachute Regt. overran an outpost recently established by a company of the 4th Division at La Pompe. The US infantry fell back to the positions of the 78th Armored Field Artillery Battalion. Two batteries of M7 105mm self-propelled guns, supported by four M10 tank destroyers held back the German attack with direct fire until reinforced by an armored infantry company. Although small groups of German infantry managed

Lead elements of the CCB, 2nd Armored Division seized the bridges over the Soulle river at Pont Brocard on 27 July, nearly capturing the commander of Panzer Lehr Division in the process. Here a 57mm anti-tank gun is stationed at a road junction in the town on 29 July as a M4 medium tank passes by. The 2nd Armored Division was one of the few US units to wear camouflage battle-dress during Cobra, a practice which ended in August due to frequent confusion with German camouflage clothing.

to infiltrate past the US outposts in the dark, their failure to seize any of the key road junctions left the bulk of the 2nd SS Panzer and 17th SS Panzer Grenadier Divisions trapped on the narrow country roads around Roncey. Many of the vehicles were low on fuel, further complicating the retreat.

The next day P-47 Thunderbolts of the 405th Fighter Group arrived to discover a "fighter-bomber's paradise" of about 500 vehicles jammed together. From mid-afternoon to nightfall, the fighter-bombers pummeled the columns. A total of 122 tanks, 259 other vehicles and 11 artillery pieces were later found destroyed or abandoned in the "Roncey pocket". A separate strike by British Typhoons near La Baleine knocked out nine tanks, eight armored vehicles, and about 20 other vehicles. Cautiously moving southward with the vehicles that still had fuel, the German troops planned another escape attempt when darkness fell. For a second night there was a series of desperate close-quarter battles as the German troops tried to escape between gaps in the US outposts. The most vicious was an attack by about a thousand German infantry supported by several dozen assorted armored vehicles against St. Denis-le-Gast. By morning the attack had been crushed at a cost of 130 German dead, 124 wounded and 500 prisoners as well as 7 tanks and 25 armored vehicles. US losses were 100 men and 12 vehicles, including the commander of the 41st Armored Infantry, LtCol Wilson Coleman, who was posthumously decorated with the Distinguished Service Cross for his leadership in the battle.

Eleven vehicles of the assault gun battalion of the 17th SS Panzer Grenadier Division escaped westward from St. Denis-le-Gast, and during the night stumbled into the 78th Armored Artillery near La Chapelle supported by an M10 tank destroyer. In the ensuing melee, the M7 self-propelled guns knocked out the lead vehicles at point blank range with 105mm howitzer fire while a M10 tank destroyer knocked out the

The key road junction at Marigny was the objective of the 9th Division on the first day of Operation Cobra. However, it did not finally fall until the morning of 28 July to the reinforced 1st Infantry Division. The German signs on the electrical post give directions to neighboring units, including Kampfgruppe Heintz.

trailing vehicle. Silhouetted by the flames of the burning vehicles, the remaining German armored vehicles were destroyed leaving 90 dead and 200 prisoners.

Another force of about 2,500 Germans tried to overrun a road-block on the Coutances highway near Cambry. Supported by an M4 tank, the US infantry broke up the attack and called in artillery fire. After six hours of confused fighting the German column had lost 450 dead, 1,000 prisoners and about 100 vehicles. By daybreak the German escape attempts were largely spent at a cost of about 1,500 dead and 4,000 prisoners against US losses of about 100 dead and 300 wounded. Heroic actions during these night battles led to the award of one Medal of Honor and three Distinguished Services Crosses to soldiers of the 2nd Armored Division. Most but not all of the German force had been destroyed. A battalion of PzKpfw IV tanks from 2nd SS Panzer Division escaped, along with elements of the 17th SS Pz.Gren. Div. and 6th Parachute Regiment. The only unit to maintain any semblance of order was the 91st Division, which had retreated down the coast away from the American outposts as Choltitz had originally planned. Hausser's most powerful formation at the start of Cobra, the 2nd SS Panzer Division "Das Reich", had been nearly annihilated with nothing to show for its losses.

In the midst of this debacle Kluge was struggling to put together a counterattack force, but the growing disarray in the Seventh Army undermined plans before they could be completed. The 9th Panzer Division would not be available for at least ten days, so Kluge decided to shift the 2nd Panzer Division and the 116th Panzer Division from the British sector to the Cotentin region. Kluge hoped to use the two armored units to plug the gaping hole in the front, and to reestablish a defensive line from Granville on the coast through Gavray, Percy, Tessy-sur-Vire and Caumont. The lead elements of the 2nd Panzer Division crossed the Vire river and began taking up positions north of Tessy-sur-Vire on 28 July. The panzer force was able to stymie further advances by Corlett's XIX Corps near Troisgots, but quickly became bogged down resisting the US infantry attacks. On 30 July the 116th Panzer Division arrived, and was committed to the south-western

edge of Collins' VII Corps, resisting any further advance east by the 2nd Armored Division from Villebaudon and Percy. Although the two divisions did limit the eastward advance of VII and XIX Corps on 29–30 July, they did not have the strength to carry out their main mission of sealing the gap. By 28 July Kluge had lost all hope of stabilizing the defenses around Coutances. By the end of July the First US Army had captured about 20,000 German troops and had effectively destroyed the two German corps and most of their constituent divisions.

THE RACE INTO BRITTANY

The original American plan called for a period of consolidation after the breakthrough. Given the success of Cobra and the disarray in the German forces, exploitation rather than consolidation was the obvious alternative. The Germans had not given any thought to defenses in depth, and US armored spearheads captured most bridges before they could be prepared for demolition. Bradley's staff began laying out plans on the evening of 27 July. By 29 July both 4th and 6th Armored Division were advancing with minimal opposition. Although strung out, their main problems were mines and large numbers of surrendering Germans, not determined resistance. The VIII Corps commander was particularly impressed by the performance of 4th Armored Div., led by the aggressive MajGen John Wood. Late on 29 July he gave Wood the assignment of taking Avranches. The following day lead elements of the 4th Armored Division came close to capturing Hausser and the Seventh Army staff during a lightning advance. Early in the evening the tanks entered Avranches. The situation in the town remained confused, and a major action took place on the night of 30 July when Germans troops retreating from further north attempted to break through the thinly held American positions. The next critical mission was to seize the main bridge over the Selun river at Pontaubault which led from the Cotentin region into Brittany. German defenses in the region were in such disarray that a 4th Armored Division task force seized it on the afternoon of 31 July without resistance, followed by capture of secondary bridges in the area. On 31 July alone, the 4th and 6th Armored Division captured 4,000 prisoners and the infantry following behind bagged another 3,000.

On 31 July Kluge contacted the OB West by telephone, describing the situation as a "Riesensauerei" – a complete mess. Kluge blamed Hausser for his ill-advised decision to break out to the south-east. When asked by chief-of-staff Blumentritt what defenses were in place, he sarcastically suggested that the high command must be "living on the moon". He

OPERATION COBRA – THE BREAKTHROUGH 25–30 JULY 1944

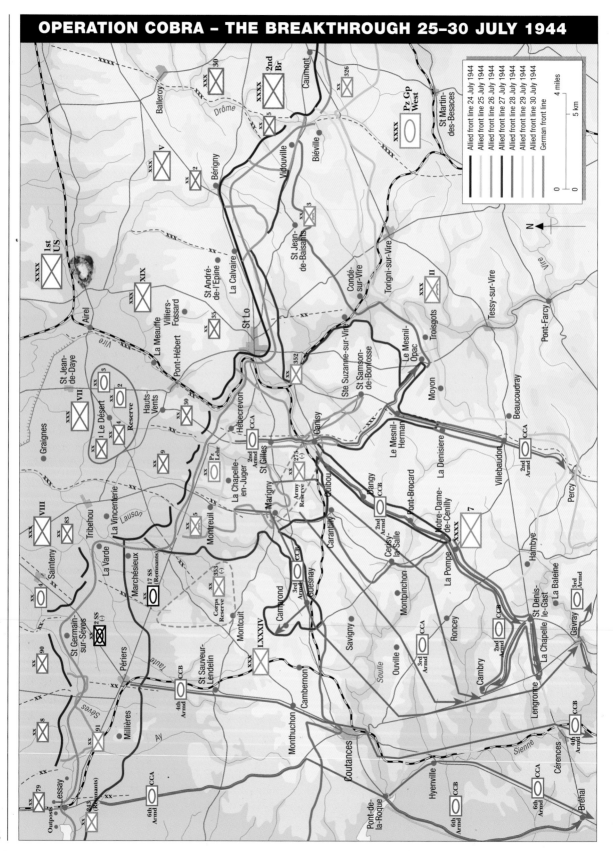

Allied front line 24 July 1944
Allied front line 25 July 1944
Allied front line 26 July 1944
Allied front line 27 July 1944
Allied front line 28 July 1944
Allied front line 29 July 1944
Allied front line 30 July 1944
German front line

4 miles
5 km

warned that "if the Americans get through at Avranches they will be out of the woods and they'll be able to do what they want … The terrible thing is that there is not much that anyone could do … It's a crazy situation." Kluge attempted to get troops from the St. Malo garrison to seize the Pontaubault bridge, but by the time a Kampfgruppe from the 77th Division arrived, it was already firmly in American hands. In desperation the Luftwaffe was ordered to attack the bridges. Due to Allied air superiority the attacks had to be conducted at night. Dornier Do-217s of KG 100 began attacks on the night of 2 August using Hs 293 guided missiles. Attacks through 6 August were ineffective and six aircraft were lost.

This PzKpfw IV was knocked out by a 37mm gun mounted on a M2 half-track of the 41st Armored Infantry Regt. of the 2nd Armored Div. during fighting for St. Denis-le-Gast on 31 July. A tanker from the supporting 67th Armored Regt. points to a hole in the turret side skirts where the 37mm round penetrated. This tank was most probably from 2nd SS Panzer Division "Das Reich".

Kluge attempted to prevent Cobra from spilling over the Vire river by sending the 2nd Panzer Division to Tessy-sur-Vire in late July. The town was finally taken by the CCA/2nd Armored Division and the 22nd Infantry on 1 August. The destroyed German armor left behind included this Flakpanzer 38(t) of Pz.Rgt. 3. This was the most common type of German anti-aircraft vehicle in Normandy and consisted of a 2cm automatic cannon mounted on a Czech PzKpfw 38(t) tank chassis.

On 1 August, as previously planned, the First US Army was transformed into the 12th Army Group. Patton's Third Army was activated, taking over the divisions operating on the approaches to Brittany. The 4th Armored Division's race towards the Breton capital of Rennes was stopped on 1 August by a determined defense of Rennes airport, stiffened by Luftwaffe 88mm anti-aircraft guns. Further German reinforcements arrived, and even after air strikes, the defense withstood another 4th Armored Division attack. The 6th Armored Division was on the heels of the 4th Armored Division into Brittany, delayed by the constricted access at the Pontaubault bridge.

While awaiting infantry reinforcements to take Rennes, Gen Wood considered how best to deploy his division. He became increasingly convinced that Brittany could be taken by infantry and that the real armored mission would be eastward, not westward. To carry this out it would be necessary to seal off Brittany from the rest of France by attacking south. Once accomplished, this would place the 4th Armored in a position to move eastward again. Middleton, the VIII Corps commander, did not immediately agree and reiterated the need to seize Rennes. Armored divisions were not well suited to city fighting so Wood sent his columns to surround the city and cut off reinforcements. On the night of 3 August Hausser gave the commander of the Rennes garrison, by now almost surrounded, permission to abandon the city, and about 2,000 German troops infiltrated past the thinly held American lines. CCA of the 4th Armored Division reached Vannes on Quiberon Bay on 5 August, effectively sealing off Brittany. The Germans responded with a counterattack from the west near Auray, but were beaten back. In the meantime CCB of 4th Armored Division moved on the port city of Lorient, reaching the outskirts of the city on the morning of 7 August. After two days of probing the defense it became apparent that the city could not be taken by an armored division. The city was well defended on the landward side by anti-tank ditches and minefields, and the port's substantial anti-aircraft defenses were reinforced with coastal guns, anti-tank guns, and naval cannon, estimated to total about 500 guns. In fact the defenses of Lorient were weaker than the Americans assumed, with 197 artillery, 80 anti-tank guns, and a garrison of 25,000 troops. The garrison commander later stated that he believed that the US Army

could have seized Lorient in early August due to the disorder in the port. However, the 4th Armored Division was weak in infantry and US doctrine did not favor the use of armor in fortified urban areas. With Lorient surrounded Wood sent Patton a message: "Dear George: Have Vannes, will have Lorient this evening … Trust we can turn around and get headed in the right direction soon." Wood would later get his wish, as Patton was itching to move eastward as well.

Although the US Army was assigned the task of seizing the Breton ports in the original Overlord plans, the German success in demolishing

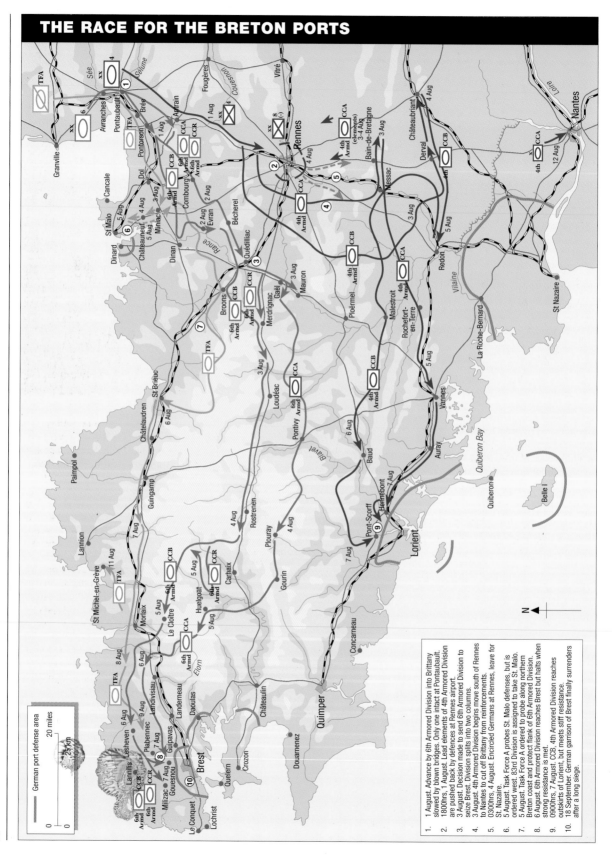

1. 1 August. Advance by 6th Armored Division into Brittany slowed by blown bridges. Only one intact at Pontaubault. 1800hrs, 1 August. Lead elements of 4th Armored Division are pushed back by defences at Rennes airport.
2. 3 August. Decision made to send 6th Armored Division to seize Brest. Division splits into two columns.
3. 3 August. 4th Armored Division begins move south of Rennes to Nantes to cut off Brittany from reinforcements.
4. 0300hrs, 4 August. Encircled Germans at Rennes, leave for St. Nazaire.
5. 5 August. Task Force A probes St. Malo defenses, but is ordered west. 83rd Division is assigned to take St. Malo.
6. 5 August. Task Force A ordered to probe along northern Breton coast and protect flank of 6th Armored Division.
7. 6 August. 6th Armored Division reaches Brest but halts when strong resistance is met.
8. 0900hrs, 7 August. CCB, 4th Armored Division reaches outskirts of Lorient, but meets stiff resistance.
9. 18 September. German garrison of Brest finally surrenders after a long siege.

Cherbourg harbor prior to its capture suggested the same might happen in Brittany. Army logisticians suggested an alternative – the construction of a new harbor in Quiberon Bay. While the 4th Armored Division sealed off Brittany, the 6th Armored Division penetrated deeply westward. On 3 August Middleton decided that 6th Armored Division should seize the main port at Brest as quickly as possible. The division's right flank would be covered by Task Force A moving along the northern Breton coast, which would also be responsible for isolating the garrison at the port of St. Malo. Task Force A was an improvised force including the 6th Tank Destroyer Group, 15th Cavalry Group and 159th Engineer Battalion, created by Patton to seize the key bridges into Brittany. Patton had no intention of laying siege to port cities like St. Malo, so he ordered Task Force A to bypass the city once it became clear that the Germans intended to defend it.

The 83rd Division was brought into Brittany to deal with St. Malo, but an initial attack against the fortified port on 5 August made it clear that a more determined assault would be needed. Reinforced by a regiment from the 8th Division as well as tank and air support, the battle for the surrounding forts and blockhouses began in earnest on 7 August. By 9 August the attack had driven the Germans back into Dinard on the west bank of the Rance river, and nearly to the walls of the old town. Concentrating on Dinard on 11 August, the town was finally captured on 14 August after intense house-to-house fighting. The fighting for St. Malo itself was complicated by the presence of a number of forts along the coast, including the fortified Cézembre island. At the heart of the defenses was the Citadel, a mid-eighteenth century fortress complex that had been reinforced by the Germans. Attacks by two groups of

At the head of the retreating column from 2nd SS Panzer Division at the crossroads near Notre-Dame-de-Cenilly was this 150mm Hummel self-propelled gun named "Clausewitz" and SdKfz 251 half-track, followed by about 90 other vehicles and 2,500 Waffen-SS troops. It was finally stopped around midnight at a roadblock of Co. I, 41st Armored Inf. Regt., 2nd Armored Div. when the driver and gunner were shot at close range. The ensuing traffic jam along the hedgerow-lined road left the remainder of the retreating column exposed to American fire, and a savage nighttime battle began in which the column was largely destroyed.

Some idea of the carnage on the road back from the roadblock can be seen in this photo taken outside St. Denis-le-Cast the next day. The abandoned hulks of a number of SdKfz 251 halftracks have already been pushed off the road. The second half-track in the column is an SdKfz 251/7 bridging vehicle from an engineer company of Das Reich. Behind it is a burned-out M4 medium tank of the 67th Armored Regt. destroyed during the nighttime battle.

medium bombers with 1,000lb bombs failed to dent it. After repeated assaults and direct fire by 8in. guns from only 1,500 yards, the Citadel finally surrendered on 17 August. The offshore Cézembre fortifications were pummeled by bombers and naval gunfire and weren't finally secured until 2 September. The port itself was a shambles, and the difficult fighting around St. Malo convinced many senior American commanders that the other fortified coastal ports would not be worth the effort.

While the siege of St. Malo was taking place, the 6th Armored Division raced through central Brittany against minimal German defenses. The American drive was further assisted by the French resistance, the FFI (French Forces of the Interior), which was extremely active in the region. Nevertheless, the thrust by a single armored division 200 miles into enemy-held territory was risky. Cavalry scouts finally reached the outskirts of Brest late on 6 August. As 6th Armored Division moved through central Brittany, Task Force A continued its drive along the northern coast, taking many small German garrisons by surprise. It finally joined up with the 6th Armored Division in the outskirts of Brest on 7 August. There were no plans to make a direct assault on Brest, as the corps felt that a single armored division would have all the impact of "a bug against the shell of a turtle". Brest was a heavily fortified city and it was assumed a siege would be needed. It was garrisoned by the 343rd Division, some assorted Wehrmacht units, improvised naval infantry and two coastal batteries totaling about 15,000 troops. The garrison was reinforced on 9 August when the 2nd Parachute Division slipped into Brest from the south after being redirected from a planned move into Normandy, and by mid-August the garrison strength rose to 35,000.

The 6th Armored Division commander, MajGen Robert Grow, hoped that the Germans might only plan a token defense. So on 8 August a jeep under a white flag carried a surrender ultimatum to the Brest garrison which was promptly rebuffed. A planned attack on the city defenses was halted later in the day due to increasing fighting along the division's outposts. The German 266th Division had withdrawn from eastern Brittany and was attempting to fight its way into the Brest garrison. For the next day, the 6th Armored Division was engaged in a series of

skirmishes with the German infantry. Grow still hoped that a determined assault could break into the city, but attacks on 11 and 12 August near Guipavas failed. It was apparent that heavy artillery and additional air support would be needed. This was unlikely, as the corps' heavy artillery was already committed to the assault on St. Malo. On 12 August Grow was told to leave one of his combat commands to block off the city and divert the other two back towards Vannes to relieve the 4th Armored Division. Patton was finally shifting his attention eastward.

The Brittany operation had been remarkable for its speed. The 6th Armored Division's drive on Brest was the most extended operation ever conducted by a single US division in Europe in 1944–45. Yet the strategic goal of seizing the Breton ports had not been accomplished since the armored units were not strong enough to force their way into the fortified ports. Brest did not fall until 19 September and its harbor was completely demolished; plans to assault Lorient and St. Nazaire were cancelled and the isolated garrisons did not surrender until the end of the war. While the Breton ports had seemed valuable in July, by August more alluring opportunities had presented themselves. A deep encirclement of German forces along the Seine river now seemed a real possibility, which might put closer ports such as Le Havre and Antwerp in Allied hands.

COUNTERING COBRA – OPERATION LÜTTICH

By the beginning of August, Hitler finally appreciated that the Normandy front now posed the most serious threat to Germany. After nearly two months of catastrophe in the east, the Red Army's drive into central Europe had stalled on the Vistula river in central Poland. The

The tail end of the retreating German forces were caught in the town of Roncey where much of their equipment was left abandoned after a series of intense air strikes. Here a woman from the town walks past several wrecked Panzerjäger 38(t) Marder III of SS-Panzerjäger Abteilung 17.

LEFT **An M3A1 half-track of the 2nd Armored Division passes by some of the wreckage in Roncey on 1 August. This is a view from the other end of the church and an armored SdKfz 7 half-track fitted with a quadruple 2cm anti-aircraft cannon can be seen near the wreck of a Marder III of the 17th SS Panzer Grenadier Division.**

ABOVE **The sudden advance of the US 4th and 6th Armored Divisions down along the coastal roads near Avranches caught many retreating German columns by surprise. This road outside of Avranches on 1 August presents a typical picture of devastation, repeated many times in the Cotentin area in late July and early August.**

LEFT **Some idea of the intensity of the bombardment during Operation Cobra can be gathered from this aerial photo. During the retreat of the 2nd SS Panzer Division a German column was caught in the open during daylight and hit by medium bombers. This view was taken days later after the road had been cleared for use by US troops.**

Red Army continued to advance into the Balkans, but this directed the drive away from Germany. The German armed forces in France had two options – to attempt to confine the Allies in Normandy, or to allow Army Group B to withdraw to the Seine river. For a variety of both political and military reasons, Hitler decided that a continued defense of Normandy was the more prudent option. The Normandy front was shorter, and the Seine by no means presented an insurmountable obstacle to the Allies. Six divisions were in the process of being transferred to Normandy, one panzer and five infantry divisions.

The most immediate problem was how to plug the gap from Vire to Avranches caused by Operation Cobra. In a predictable fashion, Hitler decided on a violent panzer counterattack. Hitler's original plan was to disengage the 2nd SS Panzer Corps and deploy it against the Americans. But due to continuing British pressure, this was ruled out. Instead, Hitler decided to use the 47th Panzer Corps consisting of the 2nd and 116th Panzer Divisions already along the Vire, supplemented by survivors of the 2nd SS Panzer Division and the recently arrived 9th Panzer Division. In addition, Kluge received permission to draw the 1st SS Panzer or 12th SS Panzer Division from the British sector to serve as an exploitation force, as the Caen sector had become somewhat quieter. This counteroffensive, codenamed Operation Lüttich (Liege), would emanate from the area around Mortain. It would strike across the base of the American advance to Avranches on the coast, a distance of about 20 miles, thereby cutting off all the forward American divisions. The attack was planned for 6 August.

To support this operation the American advance eastward had to be slowed or halted all together. Hausser's Seventh Army began to receive reinforcements to establish a coherent defensive line along the Vire river against Hodges' First Army. The aim of this force was not only to hold back the US drive, but also to free up the panzer divisions now holding

the front, so that they could prepare for the intended armored counter-attack. During the first week of August the German front line was pushed over the Vire river to the south-east, finally coming to rest along a line from Mt. Pinçon in the north, through Vire, to the outskirts of Mortain in the south. The First Army captured both Vire and Mortain, but the German defenses around Sourdeval proved too difficult to reduce.

From the American perspective, the original intentions for Operation Cobra had already been fulfilled, especially in view of the progress of Middleton's VIII Corps in Brittany. Furthermore, the weakness of the German forces in Brittany allowed the operation to be conducted with a single corps instead of requiring two or more as had been planned. Bradley's options were further enhanced by the arrival of yet another corps in Patton's Third Army – XV Corps under MajGen Wade Haislip in early August. Rather than deploy it in Brittany, Bradley decided that the opportunity now existed for the 12th Army Group to plunge eastward towards Le Mans and, eventually, the Seine river. The spearhead for the new corps was the fresh 5th Armored Division. The corps began moving on Le Mans with the 5th Armored forming the right, southern flank, with the 79th and 90th Divisions to the north.

With the German left flank so weak, and the right flank around Caen still stiffly defended, senior Allied leaders began a series of discussions to alter the original Overlord plans. The aim shifted to the destruction of the German army west of the Orne river. These plans became more formal on 3 August when Bradley instructed Patton to clear Brittany with a minimum of forces. Montgomery strongly backed this venture, recognizing that it represented a shift in Allied strategic thinking that could lead to the Allied right flank sweeping eastward all the way to Paris. The shift was intended to direct Patton's Third Army along the axis of Laval–Le Mans–Chartres. Initial planning began for an airborne landing near Chartres to keep open the Paris–Orléans gap, an action which later proved unnecessary.

The capture of Avranches left many German units surrounded along the coast. A familiar sight was large numbers of prisoners of war like these being marched down a nearby country road on 2 August 1944.

The cavalry served a vital role in the exploitation phase of Cobra racing through gaps into the German rear areas. Here an M8 armored car of the 42nd Cavalry Recon Squadron, 2nd Cavalry Group receives a warm welcome in Brehal on the northern approaches to Avranches on 2 August 1944.

The immediate tactical issue became whether to direct Haislip's XV Corps south-east, or directly east. Patton was ordered to secure a 60-mile stretch along the Mayenne river from Mayenne to Château-Gontier using the Loire river to protect his right flank. A third corps was added to Patton's Third Army to help accomplish this, with the new XX Corps being assigned to secure the right flank. Patton warned Haislip that he might expect orders to move north or north-east if opportunities presented themselves, and the rule of the day was "Don't stop". Pockets of resistance were to be bypassed, and the French FFI was given the assignment of harassing and tying down isolated German garrisons. Patton hoped to use the XIXth Tactical Air Command to serve as aerial cavalry, keeping an eye on his flanks for any unexpected German counter-actions. The cities of Mayenne and Laval fell with minimal resistance, and it became obvious that German forces in the area were disorganized. On 5 August Patton was given permission to take Le Mans.

Kluge was unwilling to let Le Mans fall as easily as Laval, since the area contained rear elements of the Seventh Army and critical supply and fuel dumps. The 708th Division and lead elements of the fresh 9th Panzer Division were moved to defensive positions along the Mayenne river. The spearhead of the 90th Division ran into the German forces near Aron on 6 August. The 90th Division had come out of Normandy with a bad reputation and was widely regarded as the worst US division in France. To rectify its problems Bradley had replaced the divisional commander, and it was now headed by a first-rate officer, MajGen Raymond McLain. Leading the 90th Division assault was an aggressive commander, BrigGen William Weaver. When confronted by strong German defenses, Weaver exploited the speed of attached elements of the 106th Cavalry Group to look for new avenues of approach. In two days of fighting Weaver's task force had pushed to the outskirts of Le Mans, decimating the reconnaissance battalion of the 9th Panzer Division and a regiment of the 708th Division, and taking 1,200 prisoners. The 79th Division accelerated its own drive by motorizing one of its regiments, and Le Mans was entered by US troops in the afternoon of 8 August. To the south of the infantry

THE PANZER COUNTERATTACK AT MORTAIN, 7 AUGUST 1944

Allied air cover made it very difficult for the Germans to mass armor for the counterattack towards Avranches. The 1st SS Panzer Division made the move late on 6 August, with some of the tanks of SS Panzer Regiment 1 not arriving until after dawn, as seen here. Camouflage was essential in Normandy for defense against air attack, and most German tanks were carefully covered with foliage and tree branches prior to any movement. This often became dislodged during the transit, and would sometimes be thinned out prior to an attack to prevent branches from covering up telescopic gun sights and vital periscopes. SS Panzer Regiment 1 was equipped with a variety of types, including some of the early Ausf. G version of the Panther tank as seen here. These were still coated with *zimmerit* anti-magnetic paste, a useless feature in France as the Allies did not use magnetic anti-tank grenades. (Tony Bryan)

divisions, the 5th Armored Division had advanced with little opposition, moving so quickly that its main problem was a growing lack of fuel. By 8 August the 5th Armored Division was on the eastern side of Le Mans cutting off the retreat of any remaining German troops.

The advance of Haislip's XV Corps clarified the strategic picture. It was becoming obvious that the German forces lacked the strength to contest the Third Army's advance. Patton wanted to continue to push eastward towards the Paris–Orléans gap. Montgomery, likewise, saw the strategic opportunity and began steps to launch offensive operations towards Falaise in the south using the fresh First Canadian Army. Montgomery felt that the Germans had no alternative but to withdraw to the Seine, and should they begin to do so his forces had to be ready to pursue them, to turn an orderly withdrawal into a rout. Bradley expected that the Germans would react in their usual fashion and launch a counterattack, probably from the Domfront area.

Preparations for Operation Lüttich were delayed a day, from 6 August to 7 August, due to logistical problems. Expectations for the counteroffensive were starkly different in France than at Hitler's headquarters. Hitler's exaggerated expectations were evident in his order: "The decision in the battle of France depends on the success of the (Avranches) attack. The OB West has a unique opportunity which will never repeat to drive into an extremely exposed enemy area and thereby to change the situation completely." Kluge held more realistic expectations that the operation might provide some breathing space for an orderly retreat behind the Seine river. During a phone conversation with Kluge on 6 August, Hitler promised to release 60 Panther tanks held in reserve in the Paris area, as well as 80 PzKpfw IV tanks from the 11th Panzer Div. in southern France. While welcome, these would not be available for the initial effort, and were a pitiful reminder of the poverty of German reserves in France.

The FFI French resistance movement provided invaluable aid in the Brittany campaign isolating German garrisons and providing intelligence. This is an FFI unit assisting the US Army in patrolling the outskirts of the port of Lorient in August 1944.

It quickly became clear that the German garrison in the old fortified port of St. Malo would not give up easily. This led to the first protracted siege in Brittany. Here GIs from the 331st Infantry are engaged in street fighting in the town on 8 August.

While Bradley and Hodges both anticipated a counterattack in the Domfront–Mortain area, they had little advance warning on the time or size of the assault. On 6 August Allied tactical aircraft noted a build-up of German armor to the northeast of Mortain. In addition, the Allied codebreakers had intercepted a Luftwaffe message regarding the support of Operation Lüttich which indicated that five panzer divisions were to strike from Sourdeval and Mortain with an initial objective of the Brecey–Montigny road. The Ultra decrypt formed the basis for an alert at 1700 on 6 August.

Mortain and the surrounding area had been occupied late on 6 August by the US 30th Division. Around midnight of 6/7 August the division received a warning from VII Corps HQ that the Germans might counterattack near Mortain the following day and they were to assume a defensive posture. The warning came too late for much action. The division had already deployed two of its regiments, the 117th Infantry in and around St. Barthelemy and the 120th Infantry in Mortain itself.

German preparations for the attack were far from complete. Around 22.00hrs on 6 August the 47th Panzer Corps commander, Gen Hans von Funck, telephoned Hausser requesting a postponement of the attack. The 1st SS Panzer Division had been late in arriving and would not reach its start point on time. Funck also demanded that Hausser relieve the commander of the 116th Panzer Division, GenLt Gerhard Graf von Schwerin, who had failed to dispatch a tank battalion to the 2nd Panzer Division. Knowing of Hitler's great expectations for the attack, Hausser refused to postpone the attack, but delayed the start two hours until midnight. A total of about 120 panzers were available for the attack as well as 32 assault guns and tank destroyers.

Operation Lüttich began shortly after midnight without a preliminary artillery bombardment. As was common in the area a dense

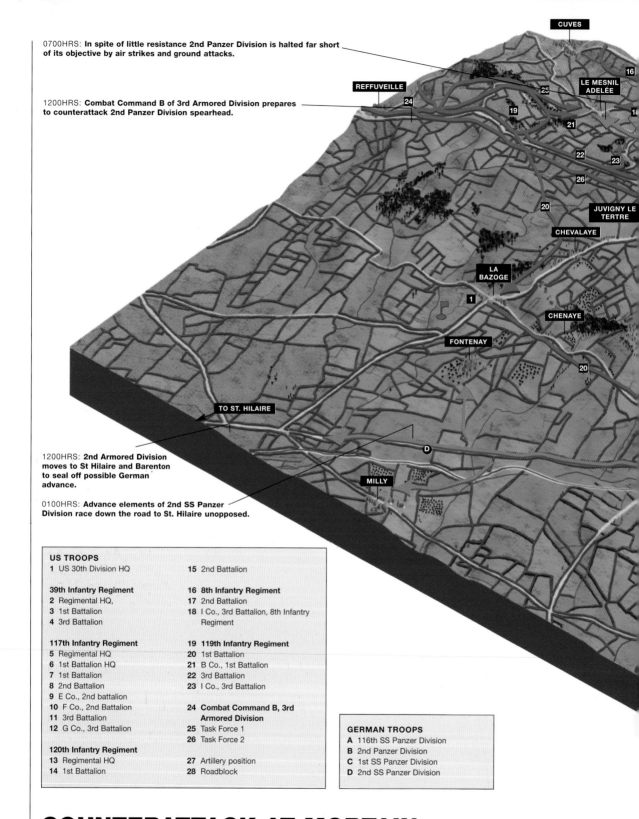

0700HRS: **In spite of little resistance 2nd Panzer Division is halted far short of its objective by air strikes and ground attacks.**

1200HRS: **Combat Command B of 3rd Armored Division prepares to counterattack 2nd Panzer Division spearhead.**

1200HRS: **2nd Armored Division moves to St Hilaire and Barenton to seal off possible German advance.**

0100HRS: **Advance elements of 2nd SS Panzer Division race down the road to St. Hilaire unopposed.**

CUVES

REFFUVEILLE

LE MESNIL ADELÉE

JUVIGNY LE TERTRE

CHEVALAYE

LA BAZOGE

CHENAYE

FONTENAY

TO ST. HILAIRE

MILLY

US TROOPS

1 US 30th Division HQ

39th Infantry Regiment
2 Regimental HQ,
3 1st Battalion
4 3rd Battalion

117th Infantry Regiment
5 Regimental HQ
6 1st Battalion HQ
7 1st Battalion
8 2nd Battalion
9 E Co., 2nd battalion
10 F Co., 2nd Battalion
11 3rd Battalion
12 G Co., 3rd Battalion

120th Infantry Regiment
13 Regimental HQ
14 1st Battalion

15 2nd Battalion

16 8th Infantry Regiment
17 2nd Battalion
18 I Co., 3rd Battalion, 8th Infantry
   Regiment

19 119th Infantry Regiment
20 1st Battalion
21 B Co., 1st Battalion
22 3rd Battalion
23 I Co., 3rd Battalion

**24 Combat Command B, 3rd
   Armored Division**
25 Task Force 1
26 Task Force 2

27 Artillery position
28 Roadblock

GERMAN TROOPS
A 116th SS Panzer Division
B 2nd Panzer Division
C 1st SS Panzer Division
D 2nd SS Panzer Division

COUNTERATTACK AT MORTAIN

7 August 1944, viewed from the south east, showing the attacks by 1st SS, 2nd SS and 2nd Panzer Division and the US response.

1600HRS: **116th SS Panzer Division fails to attack and the commander is relieved in the late afternoon. Attack begins but makes no progress.**

1200HRS: **Germans troops in control of town of St.Barthélemy. US claims 40 German tanks knocked out in the attack.**

0010HRS: **German mortar fire begins followed by tank assault by 1st SS Panzer Division.**

0500HRS: **Main German artillery barrage strikes St. Barthélemy.**

LE MESNIL GILBERT

TO ST. POIS

LE MONT TURGON

17   CHÉRENCÉ LE
      ROUSSEL
4
SÉE RIVER
3
B   A

LE MESNIL TOVÉ

GRAND
DOVE
SOURDEVAL
27   BELLEFONTAINE   DAVIERE
11   28   TO VIRE
12   7   B
6   5
27   8   ST BARTHÉLEMY   TOURNERIE

28   28
14   L'ABBAYE BLANCHE   C
13
28
9
27   10   28
MORTAIN
ROMAGNY   15
28   HILL 317

0545HRS: **Tank assault on St. Barthélemy begins.**

0900HRS: **Fighting in St. Barthélemy peaks.**

1000hrs: **Failure of 2nd Panzer Division leads to attempt by 1st SS Panzer Division to reach Juvigny, supported by 2nd SS Panzer Division. The attacks are halted by noon by artillery and anti-tank fire.**

0500HRS **Attack begins and German vehicles moving north along highway to St. Barthélemy are knocked out by anti-tank guns.**

0600HRS: **Although Mortain is captured, 2nd Battalion, US 120th Infantry Regiment dug in on Hill 317 continues to direct artillery fire on surrounding German forces.**

0030HRS: **German troops seize the town of Mortain.**

TO BARENTON

1200HRS: **2nd Armored Division moves to St Hilaire and Barenton to seal off possible German advance.**

N

The commander of St. Malo, Andreas von Auloch, a veteran of Stalingrad, was dubbed the "Mad Colonel" by American troops for his determined resistance to the US siege. His die-hard defense of the fortified Citadel finally collapsed on 17 August when the US Army brought 8in. guns to within 1,500 yards to fire directly into embrasures and vents. Here he is seen being escorted to the surrender by officers of the 83rd Division.

fog had settled in, much to the relief of the Germans, who hoped it would provide a shield the next morning from Allied air attack. In the southern sector the 2nd SS Panzer Division pushed into the town of Mortain before dawn, largely unopposed, and sent a column down the road to St. Hilaire with no evident opposition. However, the value of Mortain was severely undermined by the fact that the 2nd Battalion, 120th Infantry was still entrenched on Hill 317 on the eastern edge of the town behind German lines, giving it vistas over the town and the neighboring roads. In addition, other infantry companies with anti-tank guns occupied positions to the west of the town.

The main thrust by the 2nd Panzer Division drove far deeper west, almost six miles, encountering few American troops. Shortly after daybreak, it was halted by a task force of the 119th Infantry in the town of Le Mesnil-Adelée. The left column of the 2nd Panzer Division waited

Immediately prior to Auloch's surrender the 8th Air Force had planned another major bombing mission against the St. Malo defenses. Following the surrender the bombers, like this B-24 of the 389th Bomb Group, 2nd Bomb Wing, were redirected to attack German positions on Ile de Cézembre off St. Malo. The fortified island did not surrender until 2 September after days of aerial and naval bombardment. (Patton Museum)

As German defenses in Brest stiffened the surrounding US forces brought in more artillery to lay siege to the port. This is an M3 105mm howitzer of the 9th Cannon Company, 2nd Division nicknamed "Hitler's Doom" preparing to fire on 28 August 1944. This lightweight howitzer was used in place of the heavier and more common M1 105mm howitzer in some infantry divisions in Normandy. Its maximum range of only 8,300 yards and lightweight construction limited its wider use.

until dawn to attack when the panzer battalion from 1st SS Panzer Division finally arrived. PzKpfw IV tanks of Panzer Regt. 3 supported by tank destroyers of Panzerjäger Regt. 38 attacked the northern side of St. Barthelemy while Panthers and PzKpfw IV tanks of SS Panzer Regt. 1 struck the southern side. They encountered 57mm anti-tank guns and bazooka teams of the 117th Infantry, as well as a two platoons of towed 3in. anti-tank guns of the 823rd Tank Destroyer Battalion. This attack finally overcame the infantry battalion in the town late in the morning, but any further advance proved impossible.

The northernmost element of the attack, the 116th Panzer Division, failed to launch its attack. The 84th Division was supposed to relieve the panzers for the attack, but Schwerin doubted that it could withstand the American pressure. Schwerin withheld the orders for the attack from his subordinates. As a result of Schwerin's insubordination and the other problems, only three of the six panzer columns launched the attack on time, and the fourth column set off five hours late. Promised air support from Jagdkorps 2 was even less impressive, amounting to only a single night raid by medium bombers around 02.00 that mainly hit open fields near St. Barthelemy.

The initial American impression of the attack was not alarming. VII Corps reported to the First Army that "the attacks appeared to be uncoordinated units attempting to escape rather than aggressive action." However, as further radio reports were made by the forward infantry battalions around daybreak it became evident that a serious attack was under way. At dawn, Hodges and Collins conferred over necessary actions. The most alarming element of the German attack was the 2nd SS Panzer Division detachment on the St. Hilaire road. The Americans were not aware how weak this probe really was, but they were concerned since it was advancing towards a gap in American lines. Collins ordered CCB of the 3rd Armored Division, immediately behind the 30th Division, to deal with this threat. This area was reinforced later in the day by elements of the 2nd Armored Division which also reinforced Barenton. Additional

The defense of Brest finally collapsed at the end of August. Here a GI from the 23rd Infantry, 2nd Division keeps an eye on a Wehrmacht medic as he exits a bunker following the surrender.

divisions were brought forward from reserve or reassigned, so that by late on 7 August VII Corps had five infantry and two armored divisions in the immediate vicinity of Mortain to react if needed.

After sunrise the ground fog began to dissipate. The strung-out German columns, encountering stronger resistance than expected, began to take up defensive positions in anticipation of Allied air strikes. Since the US infantry still held hills overlooking German positions, divisional artillery began to rain down. The first flight of P-47s took off

The defense of Brest was aided by the presence of a number of coastal artillery batteries which provided heavy fire support. The most famous of these was the Graf Spee battery located on the south-west tip of Brittany to the east of Brest near St. Mathieu. This consisted of four 280mm naval guns that were operated by Marineartillerieabteilung 262. The battery was pummeled by air attack and even by fire from the battleship HMS *Warspite*. It finally fell to a ground assault on 9 September after Brest itself had been captured. This is one of three partially protected guns; the fourth was enclosed in a coastal bunker.

for Mortain at 08.30, and by late morning Allied aircraft swarmed the area, including rocket-firing British Typhoons. The Luftwaffe promised 300 fighters from airfields near Paris, but scores of aircraft were lost in dog-fights near their airfields and no German fighters patrolled over Mortain. The blue skies gave the GIs of the 30th Division a clear vista of German positions from their hill top positions, and they were able to call down accurate artillery fire all day long. The German units did not advance much further than the positions they had reached by morning, and indeed they would not proceed any further through the course of the fighting. While the panzer divisions had developed excellent defensive tactics in their fighting in the British sector in the previous month, they were plagued by the same sorts of problems as the US Army when attempting to conduct offensive operations in the bocage. The terrain favored the defender and the constricted road network and hedges made the panzers vulnerable to flank shots from 57mm anti-tank guns and bazookas. German tank casualties to American anti-tank guns and bazookas were heavy. The US infantry estimated they had knocked out about 40 panzers during the course of the day's fighting, a third of those committed.

Air attacks severely limited German movement during the daytime. Rocket-firing Typhoons of No. 83 Group flew 294 sorties and P-47s of IX TAC added a further 200. Although the Allied pilots claimed extremely large numbers of German armor destroyed, later battlefield surveys indicated that only nine armored vehicles had been lost to air attack instead of the 120 claimed. But the threat of air attack was as debilitating as actual losses, paralyzing German ground operations. Recollections by German veterans of the battle singled out the "jabos" as their single most fearsome opponent even though infantry anti-tank weapons and artillery caused far higher losses.

Over the next several days, the fighting around Mortain shifted to small unit actions, with GIs and panzer grenadiers bitterly contesting

Each US infantry battalion had three 57mm anti-tank guns, which proved vital to stopping Operation Lüttich. Although not capable of defeating the Panther tank from the front, they could penetrate its weaker side armor. This gun is from the 12th Infantry, 4th Division, which covered the shoulder of the German attack on Mortain.

While the Germans had enjoyed the defensive potential of the bocage for nearly two months, the counterattack towards Avranches put the shoe on the other foot. The GIs of the 30th Division were able to exploit the hedgerows to defend Mortain against the panzer attack, which was conducted with far too little German infantry.

An artillery observation post near Barenton calls in fire on German targets near Mortain during the fighting on 9 August. Smoke from the battle can be seen to the left of the photo.

hedges, ruined farms, and road junctions. The 2nd Battalion, 120th Infantry remained surrounded on the crest of Hill 317 on the eastern side of Mortain, and the 17th SS Panzer Grenadier Division could not dislodge them. Some supplies were dropped to the regiment by air, and curiously enough some critical medical supplies were delivered inside hollow artillery projectiles designed for spreading propaganda leaflets. The battalion continued to direct artillery fire on to German positions below, and Hill 317 remained a thorn in the German side through the whole course of the battle.

Hitler was furious at the modest gains made by Operation Lüttich, and accused Kluge of a hasty and careless execution of the attack. Schwerin was sacked for his insubordination and replaced by his deputy. Hitler was in a rage, and against his better judgment Kluge ordered three more panzer divisions, the 9th SS, 10th SS and 12th SS Panzer Divisions to begin to disengage from the British sector and to move to the Mortain area.

On the morning of 8 August 1944 the First Canadian Army launched Operation Totalize, an offensive aimed at Falaise, 21 miles south of Caen. For the Allies, the timing of Operation Lüttich could hardly have been better. The Germans had denuded the British sector of panzer units immediately before the Canadian offensive, substantially enhancing the chances for an Allied success near Caen. In a conversation with the commander of Panzer Group West, Gen Heinrich Eberbach, Kluge admitted that "We didn't expect this to come so soon." The 10th SS Panzer Division was already on the move to Mortain, but Kluge managed to halt the movement of the other two panzer divisions so that they could resist the Canadian drive.

The next attack at Mortain was scheduled for the evening of 9 August, planning to use the cover of darkness as a shield against the fighter-bombers. This had to be postponed at least a day. Even though the Canadian drive bogged down on 9 August after a penetration of five miles, there was every reason to believe that it would continue. A more ominous development was Patton's capture of Le Mans, which strongly hinted that the Allies were in the process of carrying out a deep envelopment of the German forces in Normandy. The threat posed by Patton's Third Army prevented the 9th Panzer Division from joining Operation Lüttich, and it remained in the Alençon area.

While the Germans were attempting to cut off the US forces at Mortain, Bradley was beginning to deploy units to the south at Mayenne to begin the swing eastward to exploit the breakthrough. This is a reconnaissance jeep of the 90th Division on 6 August. The rail at the front of the jeep was intended to cut communication wire across roads that could injure the crew.

The next phase of Operation Lüttich was placed under the command of Heinrich Eberbach, who had been in control of the German forces in the British sector. Hitler expressed confidence that he could succeed, a view not shared by Eberbach. The second assault was to use two corps and would include reserves released by Hitler from the Paris area including additional Nebelwerfer rocket artillery and an additional battalion of Panther tanks. Eberbach wanted to wait until 20 August for the attack, since the waning moon would give his forces the darkness they so desperately wanted. Furthermore, the revised start date of 11 August seemed too soon, since by then Eberbach had only managed to scrape up 47 Panther and 77 PzKpfw IV tanks, little more than had been available during the first failed attack.

By the evening of 10 August the situation had continued to deteriorate rapidly. The Canadians had resumed their attack and Patton's XV Corps had begun to swing to the north-east towards Alençon. This suggested that the Allies were indeed trying to trap the German forces in a double pincer. Furthermore, Alençon contained the main German supply dumps for the Normandy sector. In the view of Eberbach and Kluge the prospects for an assault towards Avranches had become sheer fantasy. The US First Army had stopped Operation Lüttich cold and the US 2nd Armored Division had begun to push back the weak 2nd SS Panzer Division. Since the Canadian thrust seemed to be slowing, Patton's assault towards Alençon seemed the most immediate threat. Kluge requested that the Avranches attack be called off for the time being and that he be given permission to shift two or three panzer divisions to the Alençon region to reinforce the 9th Panzer Division against Patton.

FALAISE GAP AND THE RACE FOR THE SEINE

As Kluge had surmised, the Allied drive toward Alençon was indeed a coordinated effort to envelop the German forces in Normandy. Bradley came to realize that the Mortain attack, rather than being much of a

threat, presented a superb opportunity. By tying down the last of the German panzer reserves it improved the prospects for success by the Canadians while at the same time minimizing the possibilities of German action against Patton's forces. While Eisenhower was at Bradley's field headquarters on 8 August, he telephoned Montgomery to suggest a change in US plans. Instead of moving east towards the Seine the focus of Patton's Third Army would shift north towards Alençon, and then to the boundary of the 21st Army Group roughly along the line from Carrouges to Sees. At this point, if conditions warranted it Patton's forces could continue their advance across the inter-army boundary towards Argentan. Montgomery was enthusiastic about the potential for such an operation. Although agreeing with the objectives suggested by Bradley, he suspected that the Germans would concentrate their efforts in the bocage country near Alençon where it would be easier to conduct defensive operations. As a result he pressed the Canadians to pursue

Operation Lüttich led to heavy losses in the attacking German panzer formations. Here a GI inspects a wrecked German SdKfz 251 Ausf. D half-track near Mortain on 12 August. This was the standard armored troop carrier of the panzer-grenadier regiments in Normandy. German units heavily camouflaged their armored vehicles with tree branches in hopes of avoiding the attentions of roving Allied fighter-bombers.

An essential element of Patton's plan to race for the Seine was the isolation of the battlefield from possible German reinforcements coming from the south. As a result the 9th Tactical Air Force began a campaign to knock down surviving bridges over the Loire. Here B-26 Marauders bomb the Ponts de Cereail at Angers.

By 12 August Collins' VII Corps had swung north from Mayenne and was forming the southern shoulder of the Falaise pocket opposite the remnants of the German Seventh Army. Here infantry move forward through La Ferté Macé onboard an M4 medium tank.

their drive on Falaise as rapidly as possible, expecting that they could reach Argentan quicker than the Americans. After this conference Bradley passed instructions to Patton, and also redirected Hodges' First Army. Instead of moving to the east First Army was to overcome the German forces around Mortain and, using Mortain as a hinge, move northward through Barenton and Domfront towards Flers.

Patton instructed Haislip to spearhead the XV Corps attack with his armor, and to this end he dispatched the 2nd French Armored Division under Gen Jacques Leclerc to supplement the 5th Armored Division. Opposing XV Corps was the weakened 708th Division and the 9th Panzer Division minus its Panther battalion. The 9th Panzer Division was deployed with its back up against the Alençon supply dumps. The XV Corps attack began on 10 August and a series of sharp tank fights developed on either side of Alençon, with the French 2nd Armored Division to the west, and the 5th Armored Division to the east. The 9th Panzer Division was outflanked and in a bold night move Leclerc's tanks seized the bridges over the Sarthe through Alençon before dawn on 12 August. Later in the day both armored spearheads were over the Sarthe river driving north towards Argentan. In a day of intense fighting 9th Panzer Division was shattered, and XV Corps knocked out or captured 100 tanks. The main obstacle in the sector was the Forêt d' Écouves, which would have been nearly impassable if stoutly defended. Rather than risk being trapped in the woods, Leclerc allowed his eastern combat command to use the road through Sees reserved for the westernmost combat command of the 5th Armored Division. The resulting traffic jam slowed down refueling for the 5th Armored Division, and so the spearheads were not able to take Argentan that day. A French column reached the center of town on 13 August, but was quickly pushed out when German tanks arrived in force.

The German situation was quickly growing desperate. Hitler's planned panzer counteroffensive against the XV Corps had to be reconsidered. Eberbach dispatched the 116th Panzer Division to Avranches to block Patton's drive north but the main attack had to be postponed again until 14 August. Instead of proceeding south from Carrouges towards Le Mans, the attack was now aimed east through the Forêt d' Ecouves across the paths of the French 2nd Armored Division and 5th Armored Division. On reaching Mele-sur-Sarthe, Eberbach's panzer force was to swing north, destroying the two Allied tank spearheads. By the afternoon of 13 August Eberbach had managed to assemble the remnants of the 1st SS Panzer Division, the 2nd Panzer Division, and the 116th Panzer Division in the Argentan area. However, their total strength was only about 70 tanks, not enough to execute an attack on two full-strength Allied armored divisions. German commanders, starting with the head the Fifth Panzer Army, Sepp Dietrich, began arguing that it was time to consider pulling forces out of the noose, not ordering them to their certain doom.

A turning point in the summer fighting came on 15 August. Landings by the US Seventh Army on the southern coast of France threatened to envelop remaining German forces along the Atlantic and Mediterranean coasts, forcing a general German withdrawal from the rest of France. Here M4A1 Duplex Drive amphibious tanks are disgorged from an LST near St. Tropez during Operation Dragoon.

August 13 was a turning-point in the final Normandy battles. While the Germans were beginning to question their strategic options, so too were the Allies. On 13 August Bradley ordered Patton to redirect his corps eastward, rather than north into the Argentan–Falaise gap. This decision was later the source of considerable controversy since by not immediately closing the 20-mile gap, the Allies let a significant number of German troops escape. Bradley's reasons were straightforward. Patton's troops were already north of the inter-army boundary which had been allotted to the British 21st Army Group. Bradley was concerned that a head-on meeting of the American and Canadian forces would lead to serious "friendly fire" problems, and complicate air-support missions. Even though XV Corps had seized Argentan without heavy loss, their position was far from secure. Bradley stated that he would prefer a "solid shoulder at Argentan than a broken neck at Falaise." XV Corps had its neck stuck out without secure flanks. To the west, Eberbach's forces were on the verge of launching a panzer counterattack designed specifically to cut off the armored spearhead at Argentan, and there was a 20-mile gap separating XV Corps and the advancing elements of the US First Army further west. Bradley's decision was also based on false intelligence

The 7th Armored Division surged past the cathedral city of Chartres on 16 August. The M4A1 from the 31st Tank Battalion on the left is fitted with a Rhino, while the M4 (105mm) assault gun to the right is not.

estimates that the Germans were already withdrawing the bulk of their forces from the Falaise pocket. The Allied commanders found it hard to believe that the Germans would be stupid enough to allow the bulk of their forces in Normandy to be trapped. Bradley's move instead aimed to eliminate the remaining German forces by a deeper envelopment on the Seine.

In spite of the looming catastrophe, Hitler continued to demand that Eberbach launch a panzer counterattack to cut off XV Corps. But by this time Eberbach's force was down to 44 tanks and 13 assault guns, hardly the makings of a decisive force. Hitler did accede to a withdrawal to a shorter defense line near Flers, but this would have occurred with or without his acceptance given the weakness of German forces in the area. Kluge drove to Dietrich's headquarters on 14 August and was told quite bluntly that the Fifth Panzer Army could no longer contain the Canadian drive. Dietrich strongly recommended the withdrawal of German forces from the Falaise pocket as quickly as possible or risk losing the German army in Normandy. Kluge left Dietrich's headquarters the next day for a meeting with Hausser and Eberbach but vanished.

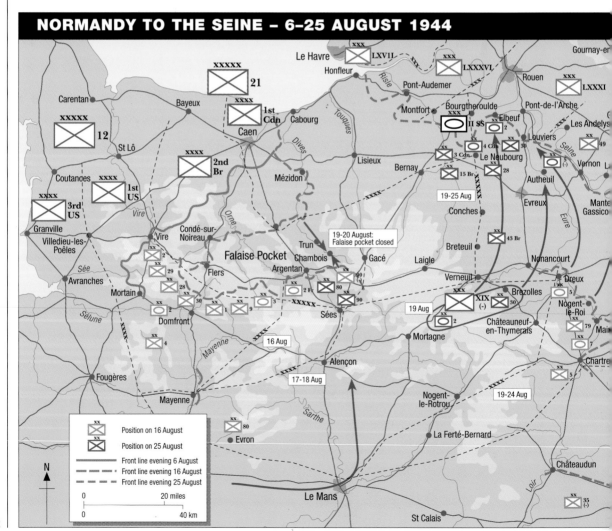

NORMANDY TO THE SEINE – 6–25 AUGUST 1944

The Canadian attack towards Falaise was having a rough time but on 14 August was reinvigorated by another carpet-bombing. Falaise was finally taken on 16 August leaving just a 15-mile gap between the Allied spearheads. As the Canadian forces moved southward Hodges' US First Army continued pressure to the north and east, overrunning the staging area for Eberbach's perpetually delayed panzer attack. On 15 August another lightning bolt struck. The US Seventh Army landed on the southern coast of France near Marseilles, largely unopposed. This would tie down remaining German forces in Army Group G, and threaten to cut off all German forces in the remainder of southern and central France.

The German commanders in Normandy, with Kluge still missing, had come to the conclusion that an immediate withdrawal was essential. The German high command remained unconvinced and Jodl continued to insist that the only solution was a German counterattack. This was complete fantasy as by this stage the German panzer units were low on fuel, under constant pressure from Allied artillery and air attack, and the roads were jammed with units attempting to withdraw. One officer

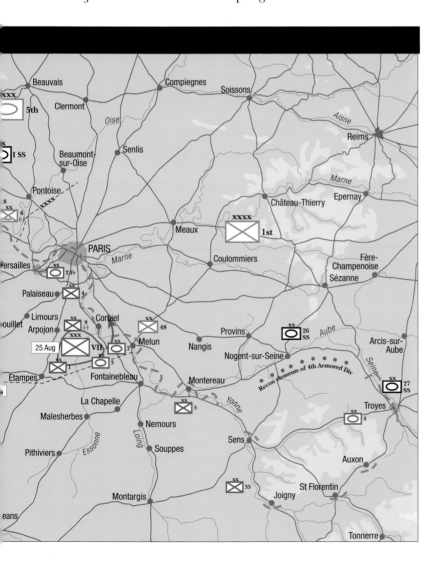

TOP, RIGHT **Following the capture of the cathedral city of Chartres the commander of the 7th Armored Division, MajGen Lindsay Silvester, drives to the town hall in his M8 armored car to the enthusiastic cheers of the local citizens.**

BOTTOM, RIGHT **The arrival of the 9th Panzer Division near Alençon did little to stem the tide of the American advance. Committed piecemeal it was ground up in several days of fighting with the French 2nd Armored Division and the US 5th Armored Division. Here one of the unit's Panther Ausf. A tanks is recovered by the French 2nd Armored Division.**

compared the situation to Napoleon's retreat from Moscow. Hitler reiterated the demand for an attack on the XV Corps spearhead. Kluge finally showed up on the evening of 15 August stating that his car had been strafed and his radio put out of action. At 02.00 on 16 August he informed the high command that in his judgment his panzer forces were insufficient for a counterattack and that fuel shortages had reached a critical stage. After a series of exchanges Jodl finally agreed and promised that an authorization from Hitler would be forthcoming. Having heard nothing at 14.40 an impatient Kluge issued his own withdrawal order. Hitler's permission finally arrived two hours later but contained the demand that Panzer Group Eberbach widen the exit by a panzer strike against XV Corps at Argentan. German troops began the move out of the Falaise pocket after sunset on 16 August 1944. The remnants of 2nd SS Panzer Division and 116th Panzer Division launched an attack against the 90th Division roadblocks in the village of Le Bourg-St. Leonard, hoping to knock the Americans off a ridgeline that had vistas over the escape routes further north. The attack did seize the ridge but it was retaken by American infantry that night. A day-long battle for control of the area followed. This feeble attack was the last gasp of Operation Lüttich. Hitler finally accepted the gravity of the situation and ordered all non-combat troops in Army Group G in western and southern France to begin a withdrawal behind the Seine river.

As a result of Bradley's orders of 13 August Haislip began to move XV Corps further east, aiming at a wide envelopment of the Seine. The French 2nd Armored Division as well as the 80th and 90th Divisions were left as a holding force in the Alençon–Argentan area. The move eastward continued against minimal resistance and was supported by elements of XX Corps further south. By 16 August Patton's Third Army had advanced more than 30 miles, captured Dreux, and was on the outskirts of Chartres and Orléans.

On 16 August Montgomery telephoned Bradley and suggested that the Allied forces link up to the north-east of Argentan with the Canadian and Polish forces seizing Trun and the Americans taking Chambois. By this time XV Corps in the Argentan region had been reduced to a holding force with two of its divisions advancing quickly to the east. Patton created a temporary corps under his chief of staff MajGen Hugh

TOP, LEFT **As the Falaise pocket became more constricted it became a shooting gallery for neighboring Allied units. This SdKfz 250 armored half-track of the reconnaissance battalion of the 2nd Panzer Division was one of a column of vehicles ambushed by M10s of the 813th Tank Destroyer Battalion which was supporting the attack of the 79th Division near St. Aubin d'Appenai on 14 August.**

BOTTOM, LEFT **The Allied pincers finally joined on 20 August when troops of the Polish 1st Armoured Division met troops of the US 90th Division in Chambois. Here Lt Wladyslaw Klaptocz of the Polish 10th Dragoons confers with Maj Leonard Dull of the 359th Infantry. Even after the units met the Germans continued to filter through the porous Allied positions until late the next day.**

Gaffey to direct an attack by the 90th Division. Unbeknownst to him Bradley had in the meantime decided to shift the three divisions to First Army jurisdiction and put them under control of V Corps commander MajGen Leonard Gerow. This confusion was quickly resolved, but it delayed the launch of the attack northward.

By the time the withdrawal decision was made late on 16 August the German forces in the pocket consisted of the remnants of nine infantry and six panzer divisions. The pocket was roughly 15 miles across, meaning that the units inside the pocket were vulnerable to artillery fire from both the US and British sides. Hitler was extremely unhappy at the recent conduct of operations in Normandy and suspicious that Kluge's recent disappearance covered an attempt to arrange a surrender to the Allies. On 17 August Kluge was replaced by Generalfeldmarschall Walter Model. Under suspicion for involvement in the 20 July bomb plot, Kluge committed suicide on 18 August.

Model was one of Hitler's favorites and had recently succeeded in stabilizing the eastern front after the destruction of Army Group Center by the Red Army's Operation Bagration. By the time that Model arrived at the Fifth Panzer Army command post near Lisieux the situation had worsened further. The Canadian 4th Armoured Division had taken Trun and alongside it, the 1st Polish Armoured Division had seized hills within a half mile of Chambois. Gerow's V Corps had launched its attack with the 80th and 90th Divs., supported by 15 artillery battalions and the French 2nd Armored Div. Against strong German resistance, the 80th Div. made little progress, and the 90th Div. reached only halfway to Chambois. This made German escape out of the pocket considerably more difficult, but units continued to slip through that night on foot.

By this stage the pocket was only six miles deep and seven miles wide. The pocket was described by an American as an "artilleryman's dream". The German troops were subjected to artillery fire and air attack. German infantry units were heavily dependent on horses for transport, and the roads were soon a hellish, smoldering stew of rotting horse carcasses intermingled with the shattered and burning hulks of vehicles and wagons. The final organized attack came on 20 August when Meindl's Second Parachute Corps attempted to overcome the positions of the Polish 1st Armoured Division near Mt. Ormel, while the remnants of the 47th Panzer Corps attempted to push back the American side of the gap. Before this occurred a detachment from the 1st Polish Armoured Division met up with a detachment of the 359th Infantry, 90th Division in Chambois, linking the Allied forces. However, Allied forces at Chambois were weak and the gap was not yet strongly held. The Polish forces on Mt. Ormel who plugged the gap were surrounded by a sea of retreating Germans and were subjected to continual attacks. Meindl's paratroopers launched a series of assaults starting at 09.00, and were joined through the day by whatever German forces were at hand. The Polish positions were compressed but by the end of the day still held. The last organized groups escaped over the Dives river in the early morning hours of 21 August and by the afternoon the pocket was firmly sealed. German units began to surrender en masse to avoid the incessant artillery fire.

There are no precise figures for the number of Germans who escaped the pocket or the total number of prisoners. Estimates of German troops escaping the pocket run from 20,000 to 40,000 troops depending on whether rear elements who withdrew across the Dives river before the official withdrawal order are counted. A total of 313 tanks and assault guns were lost in the pocket. The Allied forces captured over 50,000 soldiers, and over 10,000 were found dead. The most valuable combat units had been shattered beyond recognition. A report by six of the seven panzer divisions that had escaped revealed that they totaled only 2,000 men, 62 tanks and 26 artillery pieces, less than a tenth of their strength at the outset of the campaign. Nor was their ordeal over. Having escaped the Falaise cauldron, they now would have to run the gauntlet again to escape over the Seine river.

Patton's army was already well on the way to creating a second envelopment. XV Corps formed the northern flank of a two corps drive on the Seine river, creating a huge scythe to cut behind the German forces at operational depth. The southern flank of the drive was MajGen Walton Walker's XX Corps moving eastward from Mayenne with the 7th Armored Division as its mobile force. German units in the area were negligible but operating relatively modest forces across vast spaces required care. Patton was willing to deploy the forces in so broad a fashion as he was confident that his air support, Weyland's XIX TAC, could cover the flank and alert him of any unexpected challenges. While the new drive east was taking shape Patton's most dynamic armored commander, John Wood of 4th Armored Division, was chafing at the bit to free his division of its chores in Brittany. Wood wanted his division to participate in the exploitation phase of the campaign not stand guard duty on trapped German garrisons. Patton agreed so the 4th Armored Division was attached to MajGen Gilbert Cook's XII Corps. This corps began moving east from a bridgehead at Chartres.

The Germans responded to Patton's drive by attempting fill the Paris–Orléans gap with the First Army. The 708th Division combined with an assortment of local anti-aircraft and anti-tank units attempted to stop XII Corps at Orléans, but the city fell after a sharp fight on 16 August. Besides the threat posed by Patton's Third Army, OB West also had to anticipate the consequences of the recent amphibious landing by the Seventh US Army in southern France. This force was expected to drive up the Rhône valley towards the Swiss frontier, and given the lack of German resources in the area its advance would hardly be contested. This suggested that the Third and Seventh US Armies would inevitably join up at some point, essentially cutting off any German troops remaining in western, central and southern France. As a result a general withdrawal of about 100,000 German troops began, many of them passing through the Loire area where Patton's forces were operating. To prevent these forces from posing a direct threat to the Third Army, Patton dispatched CCB/4th Armored Division and engineer troops to the northern banks of the Loire to demolish bridges. At the same time Weyland's XIX TAC began 24-hour coverage of the Loire area, using night fighters during hours of darkness.

The first coherent German defense of the Seine approaches began to congeal around the cathedral city of Chartres, the traditional gateway to Paris. The city had been selected as an "absorption point" for units that had escaped Normandy including the 353rd Division and 17th SS Panzer Grenadier Division. It was also the objective of the 48th Division from northern France and the 338th Division from southern France. Street fighting between the 7th Armored Division and German units began in earnest on 16 August. Reinforced by the 11th Infantry, 7th Armored captured the rest of the city on 18 August. The capture of Dreux, Orléans, and Chartres put Patton in an unusual predicament. His further drive east was being delayed not by German resistance, but by a growing shortage of fuel and supplies. The speed and depth of his drive had not been anticipated and Bradley was forced to start an emergency airlift of supplies into Le Mans.

On 18 August the impending collapse of the Falaise pocket and Patton's proximity to the Seine led to a major discussion between the senior Allied commanders about changing the Overlord objectives and timetables. Throughout July the most optimistic plans had called for reaching the Seine and then halting in order to build up supplies. Montgomery had been an advocate of a

The encirclement of the Falaise pocket in late August left large quantities of heavy equipment abandoned along the roads, especially near the last exit point between Chambois and Trun. Here a GI looks over the devastation near Chambois, with a 15cm Panzerwerfer 42 artillery multiple rocket launcher in the background.

more aggressive posture and Bradley now agreed that a bolder approach was needed. As a result the objective shifted from consolidation on the Seine to further exploitation. Allied forces would move over the Seine and converge on the east bank with an aim to trap the estimated 250,000 German troops and 250 tanks thought to be west of the river. This created an administrative problem since, once again, US forces would be encroaching into the zone reserved for Montgomery's 21st Army Group. Montgomery enthusiastically approved a change in sectors.

The German forces west of the Seine were of significant size, consisting of two corps that had been outside the Falaise pocket, the survivors of the Falaise pocket, and German units withdrawing from elsewhere in France. Even after US forces began to reach the Seine in late August, large stretches of the river were available for crossing. In view of the many damaged bridges, ferries became the most common means to escape. In contrast to Falaise most of the German units on the west bank of the Seine escaped, including some 240,000 troops, 30,000 vehicles, and 135 tanks. Nevertheless, the rapidity of the Allied advance did lead to some significant losses of equipment, especially heavy armored vehicles, which were difficult to ferry. A total of about 60 tanks and 250 armored vehicles had to be left behind during the retreat over the river.

Among those captured in the Falaise pocket was the commander of the 84th Corps, LtGen Otto Elfeldt, as well as his aides LtCol Friederich Creiger and Maj H. Viebig. Dietrich von Choltitz, who had commanded the corps during Operation Cobra, had been transferred to command the Paris garrison in August.

As a result of the combat losses in Normandy, the Roncey pocket, the Falaise pocket, and the Seine river, the German army's panzer force in the West had lost nearly all of its armor. By 21 August several divisions including Panzer Lehr, 2nd Panzer, and the 10th SS Panzer had no tanks at all and five remaining divisions had only about 60 tanks between them. Losses in Normandy amounted to about 1,620 tanks. Of these about 350 had been lost in the first month of fighting, while the majority were lost in the catastrophic battles in late July and early August. Similarly the infantry divisions had suffered horrendous attrition of their motor transport, artillery, and other equipment, to say nothing of personnel losses. Many German divisions existed in name only, survivors being largely staff and support personnel, the combat elements having been decimated in the fighting.

On the night of 19 August under a torrential downpour, the US 313th Infantry walked single file along the edge of a dam across the Seine. By 20 August most of the 79th Division was on the east bank north of Paris. On 23 August the division captured the Army Group B command post at Roche-Guyon although most of the headquarters troops managed to escape to Soissons.

THE LIBERATION OF PARIS

Paris was not in the Allied plans of 18 August and none of the major Allied commanders relished the thought of occupying Paris. While they appreciated its enormous symbolic value the two main fears were that

German defenses outside Paris were commanded by the brother of the "Mad Colonel of St. Malo", MajGen Hubertus von Auloch. Here infantry of the 5th Division move forward after a skirmish on the outskirts of Fontainebleu, supported by an M10 3in. gun motor carriage of the 818th Tank Destroyer Battalion on 23 August.

the Germans would destroy Paris and that the ruined city would be a logistical nightmare since the Allies would be responsible for feeding and supplying the city. The Allied objective was to destroy the German army units trapped west of the Seine with the hopes that Paris would eventually fall without a struggle.

In early August Hitler decided to hold Paris, and on 7 August appointed Dietrich Choltitz, the former 84th Corps commander, to the post of fortress commander. Hitler ordered all 70 of the Seine bridges in and near Paris to be prepared for demolition along with a number of key historic sites. The city was ringed with 20 batteries of 88mm guns and garrisoned by the 325th Division along with a smattering of stragglers from Normandy. Kluge met with Choltitz on 15 August and both agreed that destroying the Seine bridges through Paris would be a disaster for the Wehrmacht since they were major arteries for moving troops. Hitler ordered the main focus of the defense to be west and south-west of Paris, in the direction of Patton's forces. While Patton's Third Army moved north of the capital to trap German forces, the Paris garrison sat and waited.

The situation in Paris soon slipped out of control. The Vichy French government of Marshal Petain disintegrated. The railway workers went on strike and the French police disappeared from the streets. The French FFI resistance organization, while nominally under SHAEF control, was in fact an amalgam of local volunteers with no military discipline. The FFI sensed liberation in the air and expected the Allies to enter the city at any time. Armed FFI militia began appearing on Paris streets and posters calling for liberation began to sprout all over the city. On 19 August the FFI began seizing local police stations, municipal buildings, ministries and other government facilities. The FFI began negotiating with Choltitz via the Swedish consul general. Choltitz was under no illusions about the small size of his garrison and the impossibility of keeping control of the city should the FFI begin to actively contest it. Choltitz believed that the various factions in the resistance movement, especially the communists and DeGaulle's supporters, would fight among themselves as much as against his troops. On 20 August Choltitz agreed to a truce until

23 August under which the Germans agreed not to contest the FFI seizures if the FFI would refrain from attacking German convoys as they shifted their forces from west to east.

Choltitz's lukewarm attitude towards the defense of Paris was shared by Model, the new OB West commander. Model was convinced that Paris could not be easily held and he informed the high command that he was preparing a defense on the Seine river, focusing on defense lines north and east of Paris. Hitler and the high command responded on 23 August with an order that "Paris must not fall into the hands of the enemy except as a field of ruins."

The leader of the Free French movement, Gen Charles DeGaulle, was actively promoting the liberation of Paris with senior Allied political leaders. DeGaulle argued that the resistance would assist the Allied liberation and that if the city broke out in open revolt the Allies would eventually be forced to become involved. It would be better to liberate Paris as part of a planned military operation than be drawn into street fighting by the actions of others. On 21 August Eisenhower reiterated his pledge to DeGaulle to employ Leclerc's 2nd French Armored Division in the liberation of the city, but he remained adamant about Allied plans to bypass Paris. DeGaulle politely but firmly threatened to send French troops into the city on his own. Eisenhower was placed in an awkward position since DeGaulle was likely to become accepted as the titular head of the French government, comparable with other Allied leaders like Churchill and Roosevelt. On 21 August Leclerc was appointed military governor of Paris by Gen Pierre Koenig, the military commander of the FFI. Leclerc felt that this gave him the authority to begin to take action and on the evening of 21 August he dispatched a mechanized task force of 150 troops towards the capital, ostensibly to reconnoiter routes should Eisenhower give his approval to liberate Paris. This meant entering the territory under Patton's Third Army and his corps commander, Gerow, rebuked him for operating without instructions and demanded that the scouts be recalled.

By this time small groups of representatives from the resistance had infiltrated out of the capital. The chief of staff of the Paris FFI managed to reach Bradley's headquarters where he stated that Choltitz would surrender his garrison once the Allies captured his headquarters at the Hotel Meurice. By 22 August Eisenhower's objections to the liberation of Paris had softened. The Combined Chiefs of Staff informed him that they had no objections to DeGaulle's entry into the city, and Eisenhower realized he would probably be compelled by political considerations to enter the city. Furthermore, it would be better to do so sooner rather than later, as a prompt liberation could probably minimize damage to the city and its population. In a meeting with Bradley on 22 August Eisenhower gave him permission to liberate the city using Leclerc's 2nd Armored Division. Although Leclerc's troops were to be given the honor of being the first to enter the city, Eisenhower insisted that it be

Gen Jacques Leclerc, commander of the French 2nd Armored Division, watches as his tanks move into Paris on 25 August 1944. Leclerc was placed in an awkward position during the Paris operation, torn between his loyalties to DeGaulle and his responsibilities to the US commanders under whom he served.

There was wild enthusiasm in the streets of Paris as the French 2nd Armored Division entered on 25 August. This is an M4A2 medium tank of Adj Cher named "Franche-Comte" of the 12th Regiment des Chasseurs d'Afrique. This tank was later destroyed in combat on 1 November 1944.

an Allied affair and the French troops were to be followed by the 4th Division, a cavalry reconnaissance group, and a contingent of British troops. Gerow, V Corps' commander, was put in charge of the operation.

Choltitz's ambivalence stemmed from his desire to carry out his duty and his unwillingness to engage in wanton destruction of one of Europe's great cities. He claimed to some members of the German high command that he didn't have the means to carry out the destruction ordered by Hitler, but also solicited the advice of other senior leaders, including Model's chief of staff Hans Speidel, who agreed with his decision not to level Paris. The defenses around Paris were commanded by Hubertus von Aulock, the brother of "Mad Colonel" Andreas von Aulock, who had defended the St. Malo citadel to the last moment. Although his troops were too thin to resist a determined Allied attack, they were not as ephemeral as the FFI had described to Eisenhower. The bulk of Leclerc's division did not reach the Rambouillet area until the evening of 23 August. Leclerc decided to switch the direction of his assault from the Rambouillet–Versailles axis to the Arpajon–Paris axis against Gerow's instructions and bumped into the 4th Division's sector. Leclerc's lead elements penetrated the German defenses on the morning of 24 August and by midday were on the outskirts of the city near the Pont de Sevres. The main obstruction to the armored column was the swarm of enthusiastic Parisians who had come out to greet them. Leclerc had divided his division into its three constituent combat commands, which moved into the city along different axes.

By the afternoon of 24 August Bradley and the American commanders were becoming impatient with the slow pace of Leclerc's attack and decided to commit the 4th Division to prod Leclerc. The measured pace of the assault was due in part to the reluctance of the French troops to needlessly damage the city and its environs, but a major obstacle was the continued and unexpected German resistance. The French 2nd Armored Division suffered over 300 casualties and lost 35 tanks, six self-propelled guns, and 111 other vehicles during the fighting in the outskirts of Paris. Leclerc also had considerable difficulty communicating with his forward detachments. To speed things up, on the night of 24 August he dispatched a small combat team to enter the city from the south which reached the Hotel de Ville. That night Choltitz ordered Aulock to withdraw behind the Seine and the German defenses began to evaporate as it became clear that the Allies planned to take the city.

On 25 August Leclerc's troops seized the western half of Paris while a motorized column from the 4th Division took the eastern side. An American infantry detachment screened by the 102nd Cavalry Group reached Nôtre Dame cathedral around noon, their commander reporting that the only check on their advance was "the enormous crowd of Parisians welcoming the troops." There was more skirmishing in the center of the city, especially around some of the principal government buildings where there were groups of entrenched German troops. To minimize the risk of major combat breaking out a detachment was sent to seize the Hotel Meurice and demand Choltitz's surrender. After a short skirmish an excited young officer burst into Choltitz's office and shouted "Do you speak German?" to which Choltitz replied "Probably better than you!" Choltitz was taken to Leclerc and the commander of the Paris FFI where he signed a formal act of capitulation. For the rest of the day small groups of French and German officers traveled around the city with copies of the order. V Corps captured about 10,000 troops in the city.

Relations between Leclerc and Gerow were testy and Gerow sent a sharp note during the afternoon reminding the French commander that he was still under his command not DeGaulle's. The American commanders were concerned that if Leclerc's division became entangled in Paris it would be of little value in defending the city against German attacks. An impromptu parade through the city to mark DeGaulle's entry was a bone of contention. American officers were concerned about the amount of random shooting occurring in the city and the presence of 2,600 German troops in the Bois de Boulogne could not be ignored. The last Germans pockets in the Bois de Boulogne finally surrendered shortly before the parade began. The continuing turmoil in the capital led DeGaulle to ask Eisenhower to allow the 2nd Armored Division to remain in the city. Bradley was not happy with the idea of wasting a fully equipped armored division for garrison duty, especially as it was already involved in pushing the Germans out of the northern suburbs of the city near Le Bourget airport. As an alternative Eisenhower decided to have a US division, Barton's 4th Infantry Division, march through the city on its way to the front as a firm reminder that DeGaulle was fully backed by the Allies. In a less publicized move Bradley also agreed to shift the 2nd French Armored Division back to Patton's Third Army as by this stage relations between Leclerc and Gerow were frigid. It was a wise move and Leclerc's division would put in a brilliant performance a month later in the Lorraine campaign under the command of the more sympathetic Haislip.

As Hitler had foreseen the loss of Paris meant the loss of France. By the end of August Allied forces were racing into the Netherlands and Belgium. By mid-September the US Seventh Army advanced from southern France and met Patton's Third Army near Dijon, creating a continuous Allied front from the English channel to the Mediterranean. A month after liberating Paris US troops had penetrated the Siegfried line near the city of Aachen, entering Germany itself for the first time.

FURTHER READING

While the Normandy campaign has been the subject of endless books much of the material deals with the amphibious landings on 6 June 1944, with far less coverage of the subsequent fighting. Of the Allied sectors the British operations have seen the larger number of publications, with extensive coverage of the many attempted offensives in the Caen sector. Controversy over the Falaise Gap has been a staple of popular histories of the war, many of the accounts being sensationalistic clap-trap.

By far the most thorough account of the Cobra campaign is the US Army's official history listed below, and the new Carafano book provides a fresher perspective on the initial phase of the campaign. These operations are covered in many US Army unit histories, with particularly good coverage available on the 2nd Armored Division and the 30th Infantry Division's roles. For those interested in armored combat there were a series of studies done of US armor operations in World War II at the Armor School at Ft. Knox in the late 1940s. These include studies of the 2nd, 3rd, 4th, and 6th Armored Division's operations in Normandy in July–August 1944. Copies are available in several US archives, though I used those at the Military History Institute (MHI) at the US Army War College in Carlisle, PA. Often overlooked, there are many fine French-language accounts of US operations in 1944. Some regional histories provide particularly vivid and detailed descriptions of particular actions, such as the recent book by Fabrice Avoie, *La Liberation de Marolles les Brauts* which covers the clash of the US 5th Armored Division and the 9th Panzer Division near Alençon. There is also excellent coverage of the sieges of the Breton ports such as Philippe Lamarque's recent *Bretagne: Brest et la guerre*.

A superb resource for historians interested in the German side of this campaign are the many interviews conducted with senior German commanders after the war by the US Army, totaling several hundred pages on Operation Cobra alone. These are available both at the US National Archives in College Park, MD, and at the MHI. These include detailed accounts by Seventh Army commander Paul Hausser, his chief of staff Rudolf Gersdorff, the commander of Panzergruppe West, Heinz Eberbach, and many of the divisional commanders including Fritz Bayerlein of Panzer Lehr, Heinrich Luettwitz of 2nd Panzer, Edgar Feuchtinger of 21st Panzer, and Gerhard Mueller of 116th Panzer Division.

Mark Bando, *Breakout at Normandy: The 2nd Armored Division in the Land of the Dead* (MBI, 1999). A detailed look at the savage battle to seal the Roncey pocket from the perspective of the US veterans.

Georges Bernage, G. Cadel, *Cobra: La Battaille Decisive/La Guerre des GI's* (Heimdal, 1984). The best photographic depiction of Operation Cobra in any language.

Martin Blumenson, *Breakout and Pursuit* (US GPO, 1961). This official US Army history remains the best single volume on US Army operations from Cobra through the liberation of Paris.

James Carafano, *After D-Day: Operation Cobra and the Normandy Breakout* (L. Rienner, 2000). The best recent study of Cobra, primarily from the American perspective.

Alwyn Featherston, *Battle for Mortain* (Presidio, 1993). Originally published as *Saving the Breakout*, this is a detailed study of the 30th Division's defense against the Avranches counteroffensive.

Ian Gooderson, *Air Power at the Battlefront: Allied Close Air Support in Europe 1943–45* (Frank Cass, 1998). An intriguing new look at the effectiveness of close air support with good coverage of the Normandy controversies.

Russell Hart, *Clash of Arms: How the Allies Won in Normandy* (L. Reinner, 2000). A superb recent study comparing the combat performance of the US, British, Canadian, and German armies in Normandy.

Robert Hewitt, *Work Horse of the Western Front: The Story of the 30th Infantry Div.* (Infantry Journal, 1946). One of the best US divisional histories from the war covering a unit central in this book. It is now available in a reprint.

Eric Lefevre, *Panzers in Normandy: Then and Now* (After the Battle, 1983). An encyclopedic look at German panzer units in the Normandy campaign, mixing historic photos with views of the same scene today.

Jean-Claude Perrigault, *La Panzer Lehr Division* (Heimdal, 1995). A heavily illustrated and detailed history of the Panzer Lehr Division from the French publisher Heimdal, in their growing series of German panzer division histories.

Walter Warlimont, *Inside Hitler's Headquarters* (Presidio, 1996). This English translation of the memoirs of the deputy chief of operations of the German high command provides a first-hand account of Hitler's deliberations in the Wolf's Lair during the Normandy operation.

INDEX

95